W9-DIR-649

THE CRASH PUT SIMPLY

THE CRASH PUT SIMPLY

October 1987

Ruben J. Dunn and John Morris

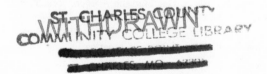

PRAEGER

New York
Westport, Connecticut
London

Library of Congress Cataloging-in-Publication Data

Dunn, Ruben J.
[Krach démystifié. English]
The crash put simply : October 1987 / Ruben J. Dunn and John Morris.
p. cm.
Translation of: Le krach démystifié.
Bibliography: p.
Includes index.
ISBN 0-275-93133-1 (alk. paper)
1. Business cycles—United States. 2. Stock-exchange—United States. I. Morris, John (John H.) II. Title.
HB3743.D8613 1988
332.64'273—dc19 88-17992

Library of Congress Catalog Card Number: 88-17992
ISBN: 0-275-93133-1

First published in French in 1987 by Louise Courteau editrice, Inc.
First published in English in 1988 by Praeger Publishers

Praeger Publishers, One Madison Avenue, New York, NY 10010
A division of Greenwood Press, Inc.

Printed in the United States of America

The paper used in this book complies with the Permanent Paper Standard issued by the National Information Standards Organization (Z39.48—1984).

10 9 8 7 6 5 4 3 2 1

Table of Contents

Recovery

Expansion

Future and Uncertainty

Economic Cycles

1. October 19, 1987

October 19, 1987. The stock market crashes. Panic spreads among all stock investors around the world. A single idea exists in all investor's minds at this time: sell! And sell at any price! In one day the Dow-Jones Index, the world's most watched stock index, drops 508 points. An absolute record fall of all time. A colossal loss of 22.6% in a few hours. Black Monday is now recorded into history.

Was this the beginning of the end of the world. Not at all! In reality, this severe market correction only imitates history. The financial markets did not experience their first major reverse. The term **crash** is more than a century old since it comes from the Vienna stock market crash in 1873. *This was Black Friday*.

We also know of the October 1929 crash that sent the world into its worst economic depression in modern time. This was started by the crash of Black Tuesday. Besides these well known dates in financial history one can cite several other dates of major market falls. The October 1987 market crash was not the first, then, of such an event. So, why speak of it at all? Does it alarm one at all? Yes and no.

Let's look first at the immediate impacts of this event. The great market plunge on October 19th was not the only large drop: the Dow-Jones also fell on October 16th at 108 points, October 14th at 95 points and 91 points on October 6th. In all then, from the summit of 2,722 points in August 1987, the Dow-Jones fell by 36% on October 19th. In other terms, this plunge of the market represented a total fall of more than one-third in value of investors' stock portfolios. This represents hundreds of millions of dollars lost by large funds and by individual investors.

In other parts of the country, the situation is just as bad or even worse. Here, the majority of small investors placed their money in the small to medium sized business (SMB) shares which are more fragile to market changes than the 30 large multinational corporations that comprise the Dow-Jones Index.

When a mutual or pension fund falls in value from 1 billion dollars to 600 million dollars over a few months in the October crash, this is exasperating. But the effects are rarely as dramatic as they are for individual investors and their families. It can be said that the investment portfolio of those institutions followed the general market trend. It is now only a matter that these institutions adopt a strategy appropriate to the situation and wait patiently for the turning point in the markets.

However, for the small investor, it is not the same thing. For here one has placed all their savings in the markets, gone into debt, and even mortgaged or re-mortgaged their home. Their investments do not have the benefits of expert advice like the mutual or pension funds. Thus, the small investors find themselves in debt today. This situation left them with a bad taste of having been misled by their brokers that so easily sold them their stocks earlier.

And now, what can one do? Get out of the market completely? Profit from bargain share prices and put in more money? Not at all! The worst has been done so why turn it into disaster? The thing to do now is to wait it out and live with your losses.

Above all, it is time to learn. Learn to adapt yourself to the inevitable period of uncertainty that follows market crashes. Learn to wean yourself of impending ups and downs of the economy.

How? In several ways. You must at first learn the financial jargon of the world. Learn about the different types of investments, their advantages and their risks. You must follow the daily news. Read the financial newspapers, listen to the specialists, analyse their advice and compare their propositions. Finally, and most importantly, the investor must understand the economy. What do the terms like *inflation, unemployment, discount rate, recession, commercial balance of payments, deficit* ... really mean and signify?

Is it necessary to become an economist or financial specialist? Not at all. The information that drives our modern economy is simple and stands at our door. This book, then, is written to aid people to learn about the economy and the stock markets.

This book has a common sense approach. It addresses itself to people curious to know more about the nature of the market crash, its causes and its possible impacts on their lives. To meet these desires we will look at the general elements of the economy together. Above all, we will illustrate our examples with those of real-life situations and ignore the financial experts' mumbo-jumbo. The more avid reader wanting more detail and sophistication can refer to the bibliography at the end of the book. Or, one can always take courses in economics and finance at any educational institution.

2. Scarcity and Abundance

In the first chapter we spoke of two concepts, the economy and finance. Let's look a little at what they mean.

In a general sense, economics is the science of satisfying human needs. These needs are numerous: food, clothing, procreation, shelter, education, etc. In fact there are no limits to the needs of a society or the people in it. Once a need is even partially satisfied one looks around for further needs to satisfy. And even if rarely, a need is entirely satisfied, one looks for other needs even more difficult to satisfy. Thus we see the expression:. *people are never satisfied with what they have*. (The grass always looks greener on the other side of the fence).

To what then does a society turn to satisfy its needs? For one, its resources. Those resources of human, financial, and material nature. However, resources contrary to human needs are not unlimited in abundance. At no point in the economy is there an overabundant resource. Other than the air we breath, does there exist a resource in super abundance? Even water which was used in huge quantities by all until quite recently has become a resource of commerce today in parts of the world. In fact even the air is subject to future commerce if the current pollution rate in the industrial world continues to increase. In essence, there are practically no resources that escape scarcity today.

We find then an abundance on the needs side and a scarcity on the resources side. Where is the mechanism that balances these two sides? The machine that tries to do this is called the economy. The economy consists of the systems of production, circulation, market allocation and consumption.

Take a simple example of the need to feed oneself using the proper economic terms. On the one hand the need to feed people is expressed by the **demand** for agricultural products. On the other hand the apparatus that satisfies this demand consists of the **supply** of agricultural products.

The resources that permit the preparation of the food are called agricultural **resources**. All the equipment and machinery serving to produce the food products form the production apparatus. The products that leave the processing plants are put into **circulation** through the **distribution** network. Money serves as the tool of **market allocation** which in turn permits **consumption**.

Thus, it is only necessary to add together the supply and the demand in all areas to attain a modern economy. The economy then constitutes a vast exchange market where individuals are both suppliers and consumers (people demanding things). On one hand they supply their services, labour, and their ideas. On the other hand, they demand (consume) from others a certain number of products and services.

In order to measure the efforts of each person and to enable the exchange of goods, the economy uses the medium of money. Money as a means of exchange lets individuals specialize in the area where they are most productive and at the same time gives them access to a vast array of products and services to consume.

Money can be defined by many forms in transacting business: coins; bank notes (bills); cheques;

deposits; credits; etc. The interaction of these forms of money that exist can be called the financial system. This includes government finance, the banking system, personal finances, credit unions, the stock market, etc. In brief, everything that we call money.

3. Economic Laws

Now that we know that an economy is composed of a number of consumers and suppliers exchanging goods and services through the medium of money, we can ask this simple question of how this all functions. Who decides to produce what? How do they fix the prices?

At first glance, the answer seems complicated. In fact, millions of participants play a part in a modern economy. Thousands of institutions, business enterprises, organizations of groups and sub-groups, each with its objectives and own rules. How do they function?

There exists a common behavior for all participants in an economic system. Each looks to obtain the maximum return on the efforts one makes.

Let's verify this a little. Doesn't a worker seek to increase his income for his efforts? Doesn't a salesperson try to get the best price on the products or services one sells? Doesn't an owner of a business enterprise look for the most profits he can get? The answer is evident.

Thus, we have the first fundamental economic law - that of the profit maximization.

This law is the engine that drives our economic system. Everybody (or almost) wants to make themselves richer! This explains why people work harder and better and why businesses supply more and better goods and services.

We now add a second economic law which says that: the more a desired good or service becomes scarce, the more expensive it gets. The reverse says that the more abundant a good or service becomes, the cheaper it gets. Thus we have the law of supply and demand.

Let's look at an example that we know well - agricultural products.When the natural elements are good the harvest is abundant and prices of fruit and vegetables remain low because the supply can satisfy the needs of all consumers. However during the bad harvest periods prices rise because of a scarcity of products. We experience the same phenomena during a year throughout the seasons: high prices in winter and low prices in summer.

It goes the same way for all the other products that are offered to us. When car manufacturers find themselves with a surplus of production, they launch price rebates in order to reduce their stock of cars. They profit on the other hand when there is a strong demand by raising their car prices.

Thus we have two economic laws now: profit maximization and supply and demand. Is that all we need? Pretty well! We have gained enough theoretical knowledge to explain in general any major economic event like the stock market **crash of October 1987**.

We must however remember one very important factor here. Economics is not an exact science like physics or mathematics but rather a social and human oriented science. This means that it is concerned with the behavior of collective individuals. Which is why at times it can be inconsistent and irrational. Just like a crowd of people at a football game or even worse, people caught in an hotel fire!

This factor does not change our two fundamental economic laws but it does open the door to some exceptions in their applications to the economy. Over a long period workers and businesses attempt to maximize their profits and to accept the play in the supply and demand game.

But in the short term, participants in the economy might change their behavior completely. Who says that we must buy a good that suddenly becomes abundant as prices fall? It could be that consumers, used to scarce goods and high prices, still prefer to wait until the price is even lower before buying.

On the other side, producers can hesitate to produce higher priced goods if they are uncertain that they can sell their surplus. Furthermore, people do not share the same notion of honesty. For certain persons will use all the means they can to create apparent scarcity of goods or to profit from a privileged position as a unique producer of a certain good.

In summary, there are hundreds of reasons why at any given time, the behavior of individuals in a society does not correspond with logic. But we must stress that this does not exist over a long period of time. Sooner or later global logic prevails over all (or almost all).

The delays generated by these economic deviations create the effect of a pendulum in our economy. In any one given year consumers can suddenly become very optimistic. They feel richer and they buy no matter what the price. The following year they become nervous and they increase their savings and buy much less.

One should note that one of the important roles of the government in the economy is to try to smooth out these up and down swings of optimism and pessimism. Does it succeed? Not that much, as we have seen very recently!

4. A Marked Example

A stock market crash is one of the most spectacular examples of the pendulum effect and the application of our two economic laws. Let's look first at the global scene. After, we can look in more detail on the economic and financial points.

Over the 1984 to 1986 period, investors became convinced that the economy had recovered its former good health of the 1970's. Fortified with the hope of realizing large profits they put their savings into the stock market that promised to yield greater returns than bank accounts and term (CD) deposits.

Good economic news along with sound government policies gave them encouragement. Corporate profits grew and attracted increasing numbers of investors to the market. Little by little the movement increased. Yet the more prudent still hesitated and waited on the outside of the market. But they were wrong! The market rose and confirmed the judgment of the bold investors.

In 1987, the pendulum was nearing its high point and was ready to swing in the other direction. However nobody listened and reason went out the window. One must buy stock, no matter what! The more one bought the higher the price climbed. Profits would come later. At mid-year, the frenzy started to peak and the conservatives still on the sidelines entered the market while the first-in started to slowly get out.

Now the financial advice changed direction a little. *The market is overvalued. Remain cautious. Remember the year 1929*. But nothing could stop it. Nothing that is except a crash. On October 19th a signal from nowhere sounded and panic hit investors. The markets sought buyers that did not materialize. Stock prices that steadily increased over several years melted in one day. The pendulum swung the other way. Where will it stop!

Thus, we have the highlights of a stock market crash. All the elements of the economy were there. All the key players: investors, governments, foreign capital, financial institutions, and stock brokers of course. A place of exchange: the stock market. A tool of finance: stocks. The law of profit maximization: the thirst for gains. The law of supply and demand: prices that rose and fell with scarcity and abundance. The great movements of economic cycles: alternating periods of optimism and pessimism.

Was this predictable? Yes! Why? Because like history, which repeats itself, this movement unfolded like it has for over a hundred years.

Now together, we will re-live this economic movement step by step in each of its major phases. We will also have the opportunity to refine our economic knowledge and to become aware of two new players in the economy: government and foreign countries.

Parallel to the economic cycle we will follow the stock market cycle that always accompanies it. We will also familiarize ourselves with the world of the markets and the different types of investments that are offered to us.

At the end we will summarize our market play. And then we will propose an investment strategy of a conservative and practical nature yet promising an adequate financial return in all circumstances.

5. The Unstable Cycles

Starting with economic cycles, we ask where they come from? In order to understand them it is necessary to look at human nature itself. For instance, what do people aspire to in this modern day? Everyone, without exception, looks to increase their material or spiritual well-being. They live in hope, fear, and emotion. Hope creates optimism. Fear provokes pessimism. Emotion accentuates the two others.

We see that all goes well when looking at the consequences of these human traits in a sound and healthy economy. There is little unemployment; increasing salaries; steady production of goods; good sales and strong profits; stable prices. No war or other threats from the exterior to tarnish our happiness at the moment.

What happens then? Gradually a keen sense of optimism reaches suppliers and consumers. On the one hand, businesses invest new capital into new production of goods and services in order to increase their profits. On the other hand, consumers seeing their incomes rise, buy more and more goods to satisfy their unlimited needs. Supply and demand rise alternatively, in spiral, towards a level always higher. One can say that the economy is passing through an expansionary phase.

The movement of this supply and demand equilibrium however comes up against the inevitable obstacles. Consumers become excited and start to make large expenditures on all kinds of goods and services. Suppliers not being able to supply this strong demand from inventory start to make large capital investments to solve these problems of scarce goods. Financial loans rise and savings decrease. Supply doesn't catch up with the inflamed demand. The economic machine does not meet the spiral of ambition and the economy enters into a phase of pressure.

Consumers begin to feel their heavy debt when they reach their maximum credit limits. A climate of fear starts to spread itself as consumers realize they have to pay off their debts some day. They start to drastically reduce their purchases and demand slows down.

However, supply continues to climb, fired up by recent capital investments and businessmen start to regret it already. Inventories of goods accumulate and prices fall: it is necessary to liquidate by discount prices. But how can one sell to customers that haven't any more money? How can one convince them to borrow more when their jobs are in danger. Supply exceeds demand, and production slows down. The economy passes through a recessionary phase.

The recession lasts just until consumer confidence returns. The time it takes for the unemployed and the scared to readjust to the period. The time for inventories to whittle down and consumer debts repaid. How long does this take? One year, two years , five years? The healing varies as to the extent of the wound. But sooner or later, balance is re-established between supply and demand. A breeze of optimism blows again. The economic recovery starts again and the demand for goods is slowly launched. The economic machine is on track of a new economic cycle.

These economic cycles always follow the same phases: expansion, pressure, recession, and recovery. Their respective durations vary a lot however: from the very long term (Kondratieff cycles of 50 to 60 years); from the medium term (Juglar cycles of 6 to 10 years); from the short term (Kitchine cycles of around 40 months).

The most common cycles are the Juglar type, also called the major economic cycles. We have seen them now for two centuries. Their average duration is about eight years, but their intensity varies considerably. Sometimes the recessionary phase falls into a depression like that of the 1930's and sometimes the expansionary phase grows into a veritable economic boom.

Let's look at the cycle that the economy has lived through in the 1980's. It is divided into 4 phases:

1. Period of overheating to 1981
2. Recession of 1982
3. Recovery in 1983
4. Expansion from 1984.

Overheating

6. Measuring the Economy

In order to know what phase we are in in an economic cycle, we must be able to measure it. How do we do this? Let's take a simple example. You have a small business and you want to know its value. What do you do? You firstly evaluate all the components: land, buildings, equipment and machinery, employees, furniture, etc. How much in all? It is impossible to say without using a common measure for each element.

You decide then to translate your inventory into dollars. You calculate the total value of your assets. But how does one calculate the value of certain elements that are difficult to translate into dollars. What is the value of an experienced employee? A piece of land with trees? A group of important customers? You limit then, your evaluation to the physical assets and materials that serve to produce your goods.

It goes the same for a country's economy. The sum of all the economic components of a country producing things equals its national capital. This excludes the non-materials like population, culture, aptitudes, and natural resources like land, forests, and minerals.

But what does this measure do? Does it really give the value of your business or of an economy? In reality, it is more important to know the possible use of the equipment and machinery in an economy. Is it in good shape? Well managed? In brief, what can it produce in a given time period, day or year? Thus we have a more useful measure here and it incorporates human capital too. Its intelligence and its experience which is the real efficiency of equipment and material.

This same logic applies to the national economies when we measure the gross national product (GNP) of a country. Here we measure this GNP in dollars by calculating the value of all goods and services produced during the course of a year.

This measure is not perfect. It does not account for example, of work done by individuals not paid, like homemakers and children doing chores. It also does not include recreational activities and hobbies or intellectual pursuits. However the GNP is the best tool we have on the richness and power of a nation. Its comparison from one year or quarter to the next lets us measure the movement of the economy.

Even though the GNP is a very global measure, it can be divided into components of finer segments. For example, one can measure the value of construction in residential housing, factories, office buildings, etc. One can calculate the sales volume of retail stores, the value of personal services, value of recreational services, as well as medical expenditures and banking services in the economy. Further one can evaluate the industrial production of automobiles, minerals, food products, forest products, computers, etc. In brief the national accounts part of GNP can be sub-divided down to very fine components of the economy.

There also exist several other measures called economic indicators which permit one to know the health of an economy. There are employment statistics as one of the key indicators. This measures the active population that wants to work or is now working. It is divided into two groups; the employed and the unemployed. The ratio between these two groups of people gives us the unemployment rate.

Other types of important indicators concern foreign trade numbers. These measure the imports and exports from the country between its trade partners and gives us the nation's commercial balance of payments.

We have numbers on salaries paid, hours worked, amount of capital investments made, inventory of goods on hand in factories, transportation values, etc. There are statistics on prices, letting us measure inflation. And there are all kinds of financial information on the nation's monetary situation: interest rates, share issues on the markets, and their yields, the value of a country's money compared to other countries money, etc.

We could list many pages of these indicators but it is not necessary to know the exact nature or composition of all these measures to explain an economic cycle. We will concentrate instead on the movement of the major economic indicators rather than their definitions in this book. The interested reader can find a list of summary definitions at the end of the book along with a bibliography of economic and financial sources.

7. Financial Institutions

Who compiles all the numbers that we have been talking about? And who can see to the proper functioning of all the economic components of an economy? Good questions!

The daily management of a modern economy needs financial operations that one is not always aware of. One could wonder that a government is not tied to the same financial constraints as other members of an economy. Does not the state have the power to make money when it wants?

Yes! But in order to keep a country financially stable it must follow the strict rules of the game. In reality, all government operations as well as all businesses and public organizations must finance their operations in the same manner as anybody else.

In making a current purchase, governments use their current revenue to do it or they obtain short-term financing like us. We pay our small regular daily expenses with money from salaries or with credit cards, and they do pretty much the same thing.

And when the purchase is large or it involves large scale durable goods, governments borrow money for periods ranging from several months to many years. We do the same when we finance a vacation, buy a car over several years or a house over 25 years.

All these financial transactions are the reason there are so many financial institutions in the country. These institutions organize and assure the movement of necessary capital for the production and exchange of goods and services among all players in the economy.

The principal financial institution of the country is called the Federal Reserve Bank. This central bank is like the personal bank of the government. The government gives this bank the responsibility to manage the country's credit and money supply.

Its principal functions are to issue money and to serve as financial banker for the government. It also serves as the official bank to all other banks, has the role of administering the public debt, and controls the nation's credit level.

The role of credit controller is exercised by the purchase and sale of *treasury instruments* issued by the federal government and by other governments or financial institutions. Credit is controlled by determining the level of interest rates in the country. This role is crucial as it permits the central bank to influence the movement of the economy. Let's look a little at this function.

One can imagine the central bank as a driver of a powerful car which can be compared to the economy. The fuel is the monetary mass which is the sum of all liquid cash and bank deposits in the country. The more this money mass grows, the more credit becomes easier, encouraging purchases and investments. And of course the reverse.

The car's accelerator is that of the Federal Reserve's Discount Rate. This rate is that which the Central Bank applies to the other banks (and thrifts) who deal with consumers. The discount rate drives the interest rate that banks charge their customers. When the economy reheats and starts to move rapidly, the Central Bank steps on the brakes and raises its discount rate. This in turn increases the costs of loans and starts to slow the expenditures of the economy's participants.

On the other hand, when the Central Bank wants to increase expenditures in the nation, it pushes on the accelerator and reduces the discount rate. Here the interest paid on bank savings rates and credit rates fall which increases consumption in the economy.

The ordinary banks constitute the second most important group of financial institutions in the country. Under strict surveillance of the federal government they deal directly with the public and businessmen. They receive the savings deposits and also offer a great variety of services to their customers: loans to consumers and businessmen; mortgage loans; credit cards; etc. Also there are savings and consumer loan companies, and credit unions that all play the same role.

Other financial type organizations are those under government responsibility like the Government National Mortgage Association (Ginnie Mae and Fannie Mae), Farm Credit Administration, Export-Import Bank .

Finally there are stock (securities) brokers, mutual funds, and insurance companies all playing in the financial world.

8. Inflation

We have seen earlier that there exists a number of measures to detect the health of the economy. What economic indicator tells us when the economy is heating up? Which indicator comes into play during a period of overheating or, better said, inflation? Let's not forget that the symptoms of this phenomenon are not always obvious as they always follow a period of prosperity in the economy.

Let's get a better grasp of this phenomenon then. Imagine a driver of a car running at 65 mph. All is going well but the highway is boring and he is running late. So he accelerates to 70 mph and there is no problem at all. What a great machine he thinks. Again he pushes the speed up to 75, then 80 and finally 85 mph. This is really rolling.

Of course, he cannot see the tires that are twisting their threads at every turn or the springs and shocks that are feeling extra pressures. Also he cannot see or hear the engine either. Like the oil that is overheating and evaporating bit by bit. Of course there is his dash indicator that is blinking but one can never depend on these things! He arrives at his destination without accident or problems most of the time just until the day where ...

It goes the same way in the economy. The periods of overheating resulting from prosperity, from the imperfections of certain measurements in gauging economic movements with accuracy, and of course, from the ambitions and emotions existing in human nature.

The unlimited needs expressed by consumers usually propel businessmen to push the production machine towards new highs. The politicians, always preoccupied with the next election date, hesitate to slow the machine that appears to be functioning so well! Prosperity engenders boldness and imprudence.

In a period of overheating, most key economic indicators record the positive results of the economy. Production increases, unemployment decreases, interest rates remain low and credit is readily available. In fact, there is only one symptom that guarantees the presence of overheating pressures in the economy. And this is inflation. What then, does this consist of?

Inflation is what raises prices and costs without an equal raise in product or service quality or quantity. The quality factor is very important in the definition. One cannot in effect define as inflationary the improvement of a product or service in the economy. For instance a car with new technology giving better performance than past models can justify an increase in its price without being inflationary.

The measurement of inflation does however present problems. If we have a very standard product which varies very little, like a liter of milk, one can easily detect inflation when the price rises. However with products that regularly reflect modifications or style changes like cars and clothes we have problems in detecting inflation with price increases. Certain companies are masters in the art of justifying price variations by changing their products in some marginal way and this makes inflation very difficult to identify.

However economists have developed methods that regularly measure inflationary trends. These trends are evaluated by different price indices: industrial selling price index; GNP expenditure index; food price index; and the most well known, the consumer price index (CPI).

Each of these indices reveals the inflationary change of prices compared to a given base year. For example, *the CPI of 120.6 in 1986 (1981=100)* indicates that the price of a group of essential consumer goods and services for the average family has risen 20.6% since the year 1981.

These indices have become very useful as they permit the ongoing measurement of material goods in real dollars. For instance if your annual net income has increased by more than 20.6% during the 1981-1987 period, your capacity to buy the same consumer goods and services has increased since 1981. Thus your standard of living has risen.

We use price indices in other ways also. When for example an economic number is not deflated by a price index, one can say that it is expressed in current dollars. This means dollars of the year in progress. However in using a price index, we obtain the expressed value of constant dollars from the base year. For example, by dividing your net income by the CPI of 120.6, you can calculate your income in constant 1981 dollars. This lets you determine if your buying power has really improved or fallen from this date.

An inflation rate of 2 to 3% per year can be called average and is generally considered normal and inevitable in a slow growth phase of the economy.

When the rate varies between 4 to 7% a year, the inflation rate is considered fast paced. Above this level we have a rate galloping out of control.

Thus a high inflation trend has negative impacts for the economy and society in general: giving a lesser real income to people on pensions non-indexed to the CPI; making for high wage demands from workers; slowing down the country's exports due to the higher prices other nations must pay.

9. Overheating

The year 1980 marked the peak for the U.S. in pressure on the economy. The constant climbing of inflation as measured by the Consumer's Price Index (CPI), hit a high rate of 13.5%. In Japan, the peak was reached the same year at 7.9% and in Canada at 12.5% in 1981.

The gravity of the situation was caused by ongoing inflationary rates higher and higher over the ten years to 1980. From 4.3% in 1971, the inflation rate advanced to 11% in 1974 and 9.1% in 1975; it slowed a little, ranging between 6 and 7% over the next three years; but increased to 11.3% in 1979. In all, the CPI rose on average 9.4% per year between 1974 to 1981. For the 20 years preceding 1974 it rose only 2.6% on average per year.

And of course, the nation's production followed along with this rapid inflation. The Gross National Product (GNP) gained from 2% to 5% a year (except for 1980 with -0.2%). All the economic sectors boomed at full output: mining and forestry; manufacturing; construction; transportation; retailing; services; etc.

The unemployment rate kept around 6% for the previous three years. This was a fairly low rate considering the divergent aspects of the economy. All workers were earning good money, some very good money. And they were spending it without counting. New housing starts were still running at 1,745,000 units in 1979 after passing the two million mark in 1978, giving home ownership to many people for the first time.

However, the country's production machine was not able to follow this fast-paced rhythm. It found it more and more difficult to keep up to the growing demand of consumers. Factory inventories fell dramatically The overheated economy had generated constant price increases and the only possible response was a shortage of resources.

Social problems were multiplying and strikes were accelerating. Everyone wanted salary increases to maintain and even improve their standard of living as inflation ate away their incomes. The retired were complaining and demanding greater indexing of their pensions. And they got it. Everything was being indexed to the CPI, even income tax tables. In this manner, the inflation spiral could continue forever.

The stock market followed this frantic pace. The prices of Industrial shares jumped 17% between 1979 and 1980. In 1981, the rate of growth dropped 7.2%, announcing a first signal on the impending slowdown. One should note here that some market specialists have a flair for market feel, and this gives them the chance to sometimes guess in advance the movements of the economy. And they profit on it!

Also during this period the politicians and monetary authorities could not do enough, if much at all, to slow this flaming economic overheating. Even though from 1977 the bank rates on business loans went from 7.8% to 13.2% in 1979 and to 15.2% in 1980.

Throughout the course of the following year the interest rate hovered around 20%. Loans became prohibitive, mortgages inaccessible, and personal credit rates ridiculous. One had decided to break the galloping inflation rate at all costs.

At the end of 1981 then, the boom came to a halt. And like all mass movements it hit slowly but surely, sending the country and the rest of the world into a recession.

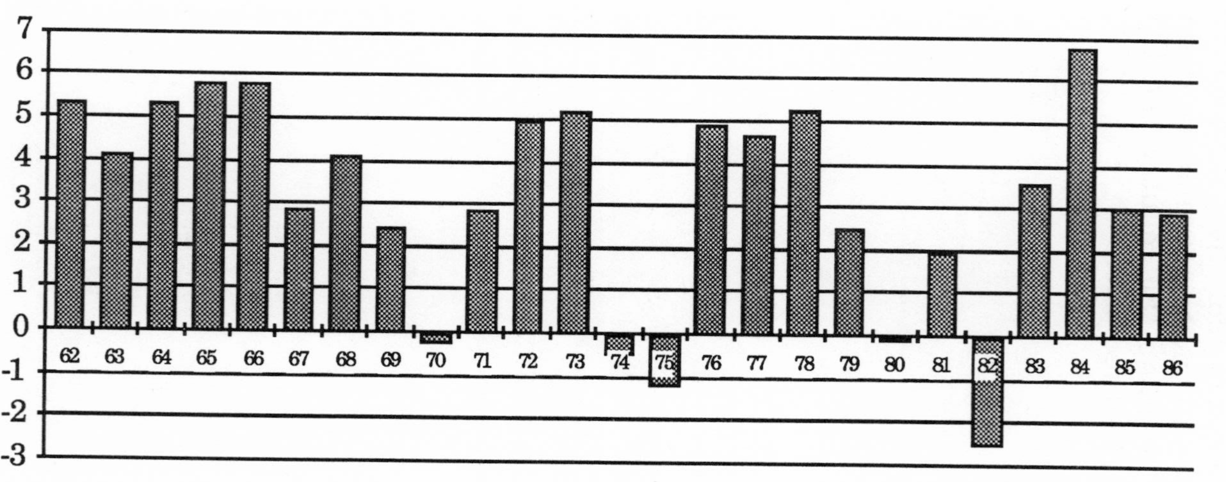
U.S. Gross National Product
at 1982 Constant Prices (Yearly % of Growth)
7
6
5
4
3
2
1
0
-1
-2
-3
62
63
64
65
66
67
68
69
70
71
72
73
74
75
76
77
78
79
80
81
82
83
84
85
86
Year

U.S. Federal Government Surplus or Deficit
(in billions of current dollars)

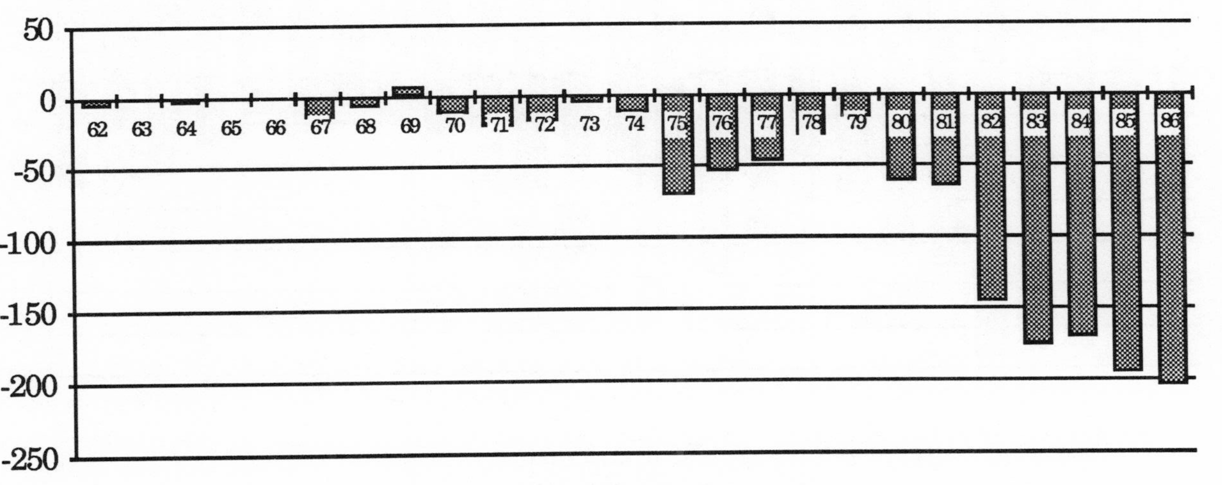

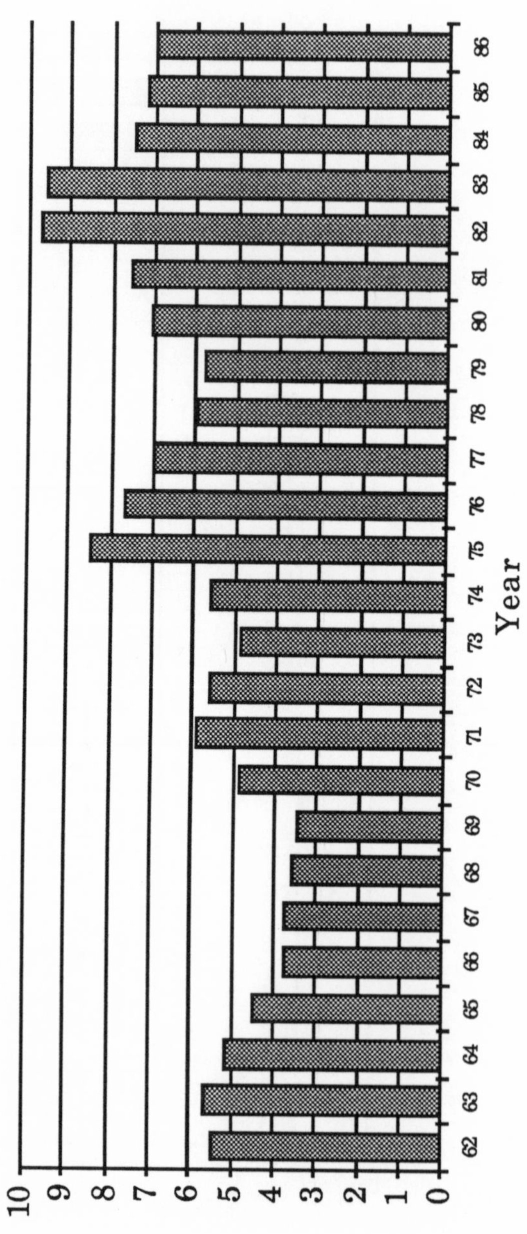

U.S. Unemployment Rate
Annual average (%)
10
9
8
7
6
5
4
3
2
1
0
62
63
64
65
66
67
68
69
70
71
72
73
74
75
76
77
78
79
80
81
82
83
84
85
86
Year

U.S. Bank Rates on
Short Term Business Loans
Annual Average (%)

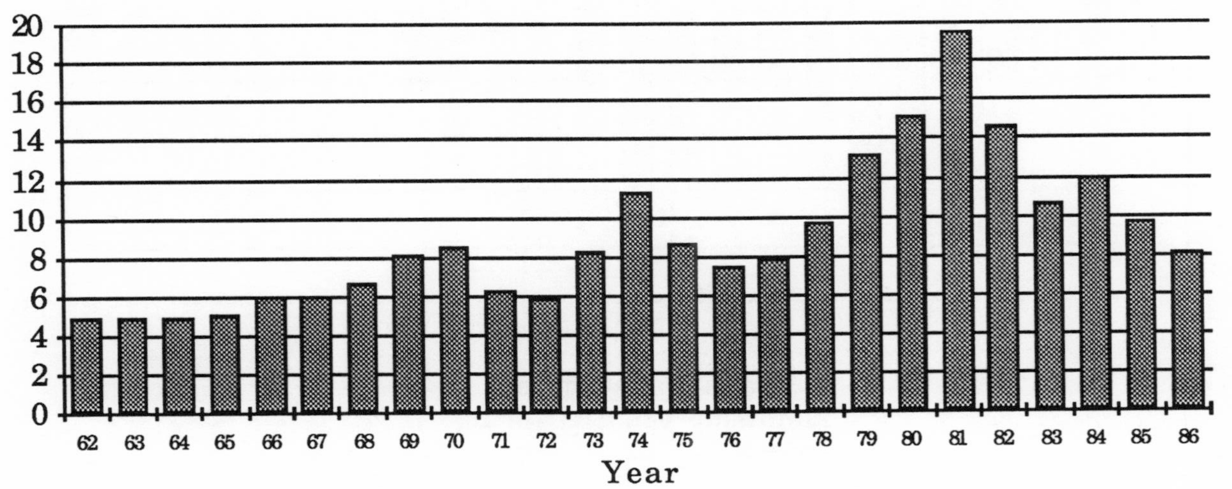

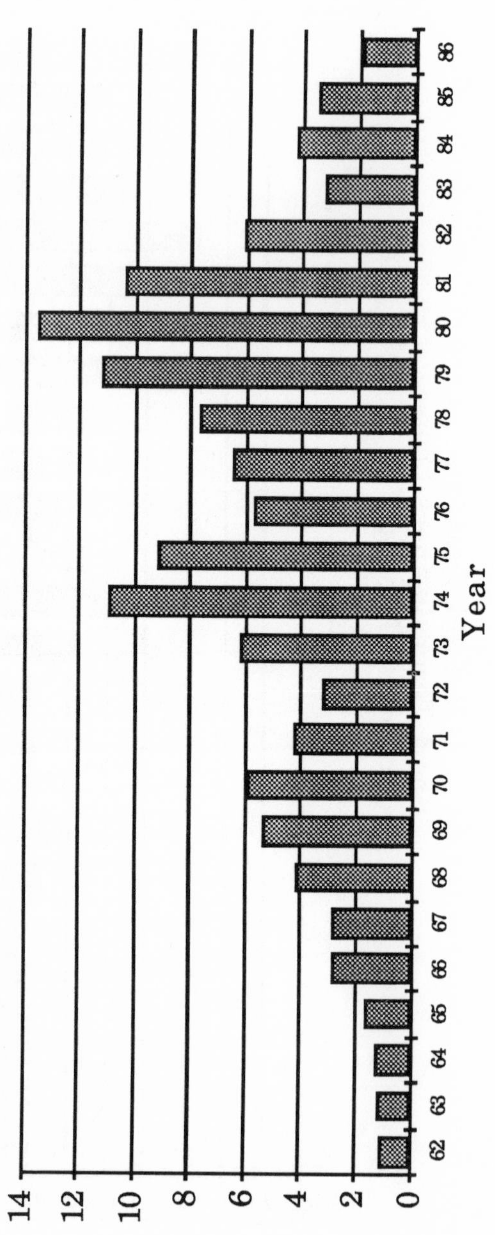

U.S. Consumer Price Index
for all Urban Consumers
Yearly % of Growth
14
12
10
8
6
4
2
0
62
63
64
65
66
67
68
69
70
71
72
73
74
75
76
77
78
79
80
81
82
83
84
85
86
Year

U.S. Index of Consumer Sentiment
(1st Quarter of 1966=100)

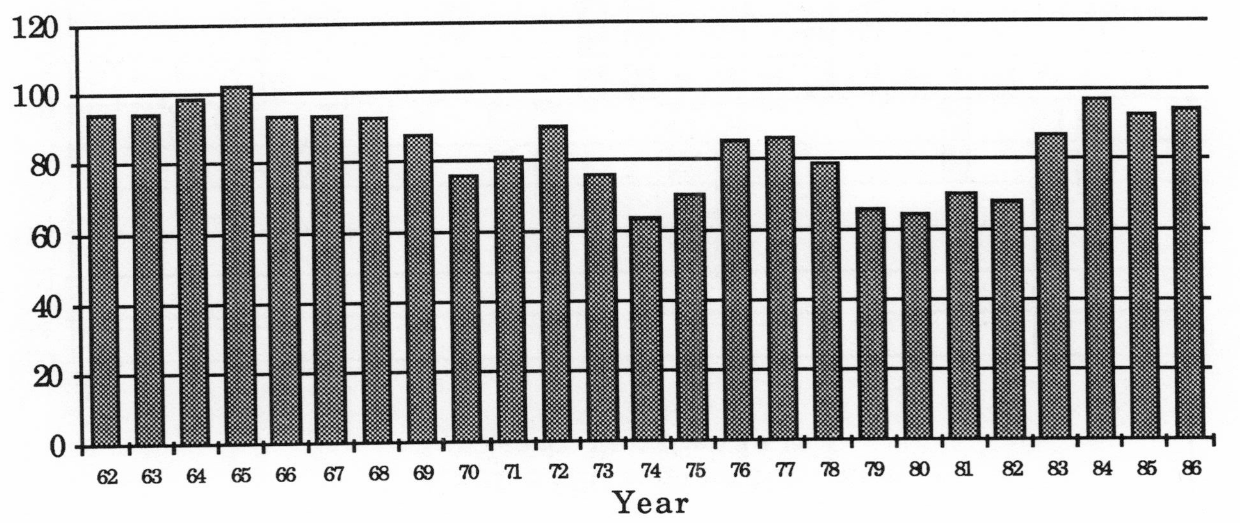

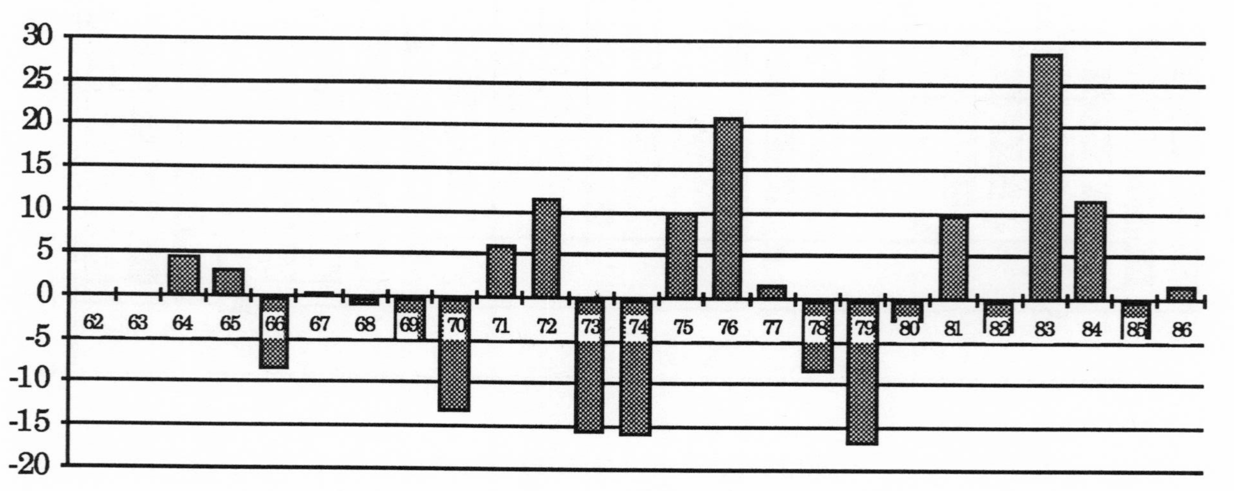
U.S. Index of Consumer Sentiment
Yearly Variation in %
30
25
20
15
10
5
0
-5
-10
-15
-20
62
63
64
65
66
67
68
69
70
71
72
73
74
75
76
77
78
79
80
81
82
83
84
85
86
Year

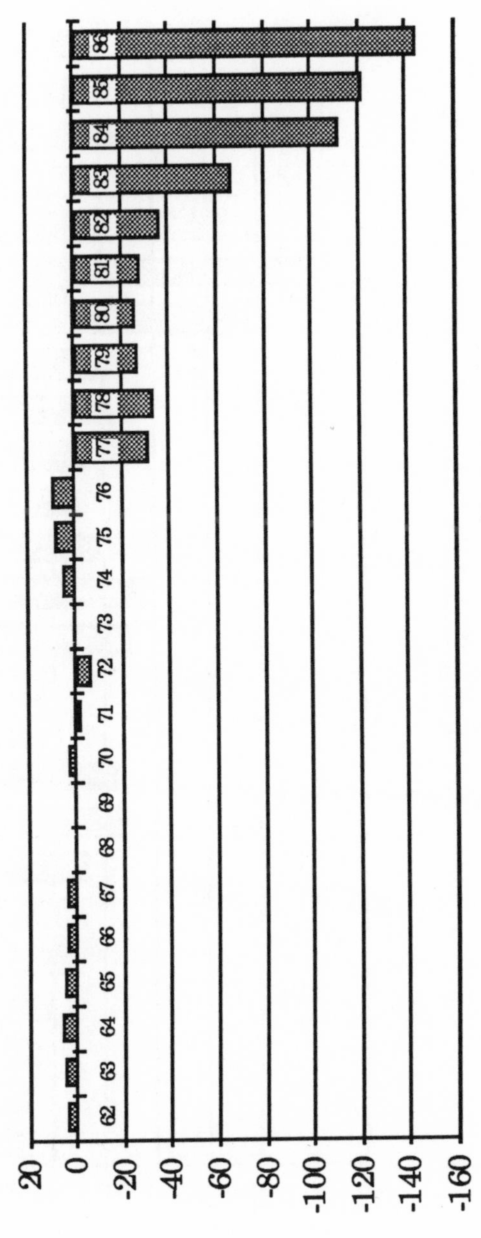

U.S. Balance on Merchandise Trade
(in Billions of Current Dollars)
20
0
-20
-40
-60
-80
-100
-120
-140
-160
62
63
64
65
66
67
68
69
70
71
72
73
74
75
76
77
78
79
80
81
82
83
84
85
86
Year

U.S. Discount Rate on New Issues
of 91-day Treasury Bills (%)

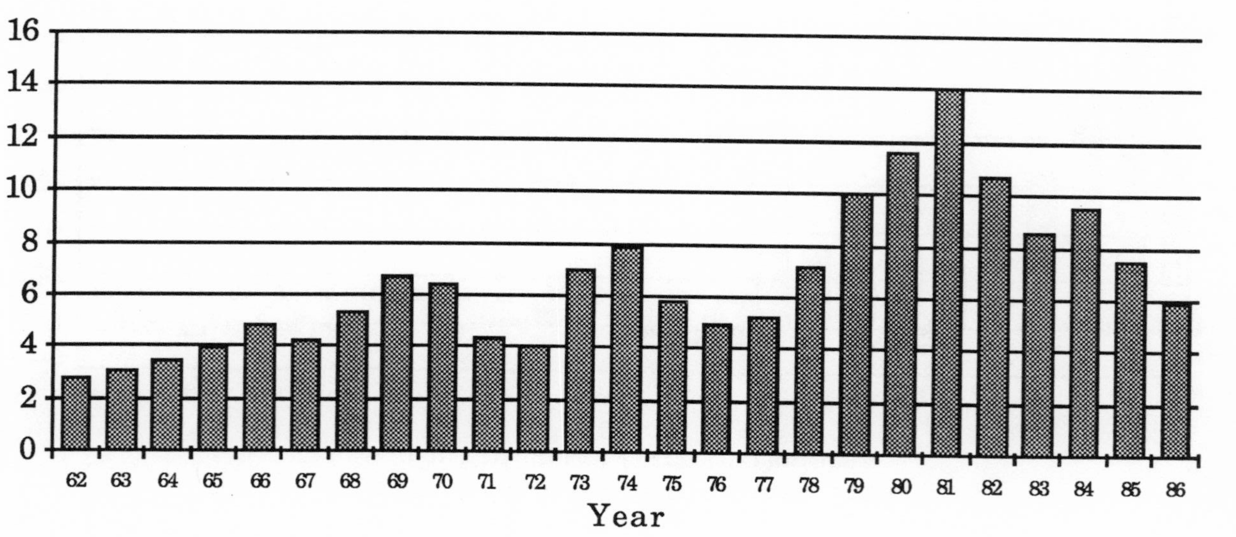

10. From Theory to Practice

We will now start to apply some of our theoretical knowledge by building up an investment portfolio - really getting into the game. This portfolio will enable us to buy and sell selected investments while looking at the economic cycles and the stock markets at the same time.

Let's set the rules of the game. Our starting capital (cash investment) will be $20,000. No money will be added or subtracted during the game. We will calculate at each step our progress on our initial capital.

We will calculate our investment buys and sales at the interest rates and prices prevailing towards the middle of each year. Also as we must pay our stock broker for the trades, we will include a standard 3% commission for each buy/sell trade.

Finally, in order not to be swamped with accounting, we will ignore any tax deductions and income tax payable on our investments.

This does not mean it is unimportant in calculating our total net profits on the portfolio, but the goal of the game is to show you the evolution of our capital under the highs and lows of the economic cycles and not worry about the tax man.

We will use a gradual escalating investment strategy. At first simple and conservative then becoming more bold and diversified. All geared to the optimism of the economic periods we see. At the end of the game we will measure our profits compared to placing the $20,000 elsewhere in the economy.

Thus, let's start from June 1981. Where do we first put our money? A look at the current high rate of inflation tells us to choose an investment with a yield the same or more. Not having much experience yet we will select a sure thing: $10,000 in U.S. Savings Bonds at 14% annual interest and $10,000 in a bank term deposit at 13.6% interest.

These investments will let us quickly cash our money when needed. For who knows what is in store around the corner.

Transactions **1981**

Transactions	**Qty**		**Price**	**Total $**	**Cash $**
Initial investment					20,000
Buy: U.S. Savings Bonds 14%	10	@	1,000	10,000	10,000

Portfolio **1981**

Best value	**Qty**	**Cost $**	**Market value $**
U.S. Savings Bonds 14%	10	10,000	10,000
Cash: Bank deposit @ 13.6%		10,000	10,000
Sub-total		**20,000**	**20,000**
Total		**20,000**	**20,000**

Recession

11. Investment Types

Conservatively then, we have made our first investments. A bank term deposit and savings bonds. What are the other possibilities? They are almost unlimited depending on what your needs are at any given time. We will look at some of them right away by ranging them in order of risk and complexity. Later we will look at the most popular and accessible types in greater detail.

Firstly, where do we find the backup information for the management of a portfolio? It is necessary, as we have learned to have information on the state of the economy, key financial numbers, economic forecasts, etc. We can find all sorts of information in a number of publications: Bureau of Statistics reports, State reports, bank economic reviews, companies annual reports, financial and business magazines, etc.

However the best source of information is found at our door - the business section of our daily newspaper. It is a good idea to spend a few minutes each day scanning and reading articles on the state of the economy in your paper. Take a good look at the business section of a major newspaper and see what it contains.

One sees information on the economic state. At regular intervals there are reports on the major economic indicators like unemployment, inflation rates, industrial production levels, etc. The business analysts explain these elements clearly and in some detail. They also talk about economic forecasts made by others and give you their opinions even.

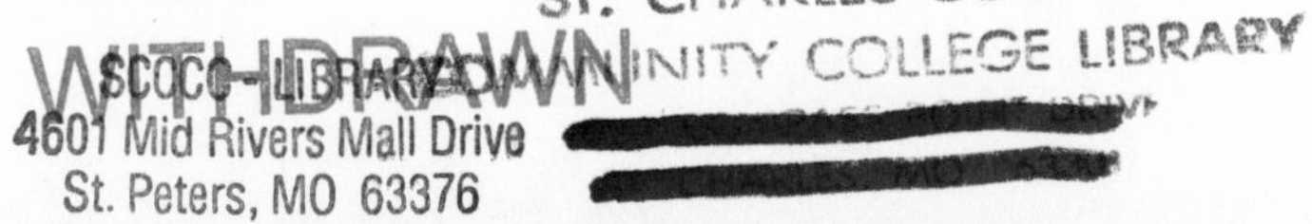

One sees particular events on the economy both national and international which can touch or influence the confidence of consumers and investors. A serious reader can quickly familiarize himself on the vocabulary and start to form his personal opinion on the state of the economy. An opinion he can refine day by day by keeping abreast of the business news in the paper and by gradually following the financial numbers.

Numbers like interest rates. Rates which vary for different types of investments available: treasury bills, bank deposits, savings bonds, and other government and corporate bonds, mortgage rates, and stock dividend rates (yields) of large corporations.

As we read through our paper then, we come across the daily summary tables of stock market results. Here there are indices that give the movements of groups of stocks on the major stock markets in the country by economic sub-sectors: industrial products; metals and mines; oil and gas; transportation; etc. We can also see a summary list of the most active stocks on the major markets the previous day, showing their prices and their volume of shares traded.

Regarding stocks, we have to realize that they all have different risk and profit possibilities. At the top of the line, we find the sure value stocks which are called Blue Chips.

The blue chips are the shares of the very large multinational corporations usually operating in many sectors. The shares of these companies (ex. IBM, Exxon, Shell, Dupont, Merck, etc.) offer a high degree of stability and have little risk in good or bad periods. Other kinds of safe stocks belong to food companies and public utilities like electricity and telephone companies.

The second important category, the superior value stocks, regroup the greatest number of companies on the stock markets. Here one finds established companies of lesser size than the blue chips above. There are all types of businesses in this category.

A third category can be called cyclic stocks where the nature of their business varies in relation to the highs and lows of the economy. Here we find auto manufacturers whose sales slow considerably in recessionary periods taking with them all the companies involved in supplying them with parts, steel, and aluminum, etc. We also see companies in forest products, construction, etc. that fall with housing cycles in a recession.

Another special category of stocks are those companies that are in high technology such as computing equipment, robotics, electronic components, etc. Their stocks have a tremendous volatility during their first few years on the market.

Finally at the bottom of the list we have speculative stocks. These are almost always new companies with growth potential, and they include the SMB's and small mining and oil exploration firms which sometimes only exist on paper. This group is even more risky than the high tech stocks but many of them can grow into solid profitable businesses given a few years.

The business and financial pages further give us foreign currency tables on all industrial countries. They also provide commodity prices of all kinds; grain prices, poultry and dairy prices, fruit and vegetable prices, livestock prices, precious metals like gold and silver, base metals like aluminum and copper, etc. These price figures are important because they aid us in evaluating the performance of companies and their associate firms who supply them. For instance, low prices for base metals indicate a weak demand or an over-supply of these products which will probably lower their profits in the near future.

One of the most intriguing sections lies in the future and options contracts. These apply to stocks as well as many commodities that we have referred to above. However, with futures, one does not buy any stock or commodities. A future gives the right to buy or sell at a later date the stock at the price determined in advance. One has the right for example, to buy gold over a three month period at $450 U.S. an ounce.

Futures are an important investment for users of commodities. They need to know in advance the cost of including commodities in their manufactured products. But, as we will explain further on, they are also a very risky type of investment (or rather speculation) for the ordinary investor as they can fluctuate wildly in price at anytime.

12. The 1982 Recession

Let's return now to our economic cycles by talking about the recessionary period of 1982. Recession represents the Winter of an economic cycle. Always rigorous, never agreeable, and much too long to bear. A recession ends the good times that we always want to go on forever. In economic terms it highlights the reality of scarcity in resources. One could say that economic progress is not without costly efforts and necessary sacrifices.

The 1982 recession followed a remarkable 30 year period of economic growth. The last major real decrease in U.S. GNP was in 1975 joining the poor years immediately following World War II and of course the Great Depression of the 1930's. Thus we have 30 years of progress punctuated by a few minor economic halts. After all these years of relative prosperity one can easily imagine the shock of 1982. It hit at just the moment where one thought the economy would never falter again. And the nation's GNP fell by 2.5% in one year. No sector was spared.

First off, the manufacturing sector saw its production fall. And it was the larger scaled businesses that got hit before the others. The sales of new cars plunged drastically and the new housing market had a drop to 1,084,000 units from nearly 1.8 million two years earlier.

A chain reaction was triggered and it spread to all suppliers. Less durable goods which generated less orders for steel, aluminum, wood products, rubber, plastics, and all the components that the smaller enterprises sell to the large manufacturers.

The stock markets reflected the pessimism in the economy and the industrial share index fell by more than 7%. Profits were zero for almost all businesses.

Weakness in sales rapidly created layoffs in the labour force. The rate of active population growth slowed down. Who wants to enter a labour force where there are zero jobs available. The number of unemployed climbed from 9,389,000 to 12,036,000 in less than a year. By the end of 1982, the unemployment rate touched 10.8%. The welfare rolls mounted as thousands lost their unemployment benefits.

The production decline also touched trade imports which fell by 6.5%. U.S. exported its recession to its trading partners, but it was polite enough to lower its exports by 13% for the year.

There were less purchases and less sales. Less sales, less production. Less production, less work. Less work, less income. Less income, less purchases. And the vicious circle was in full swing.

How long must this mismanagement of the economy go on? In 1982 prices continued to rise to 6.1% and although it was a net improvement over 1981, it was still too much. Restrictive credit measures were applied throughout the year and the interest rates on business loans were held at 14.7%.

Slowly the health of the economy started to improve because it was seen that we were in a period of decline or better still a recession. And because of the misery, the governments dramatically increased social aid measures and these in turn served to give some push to the economy.

The weak enterprises fell out of the game as they were not able to adapt to the difficult times. The stronger profited by cleaning out their dead wood amongst their employees. Everyone tried desperately to limit the plunge in their profit picture.

The workers who maintained their jobs were asked to help re-establish a competitive position for their companies to succeed domestically and internationally.

The economy would win, as long as Spring is not far behind.

13. Bonds

In order to enrich our investment strategy we will now look in greater detail at bonds as a new financial tool.

A bond is a title of assets sold to an investor (holder) and guaranteed directly by the assets of this borrower. To an extent, one can compare bonds to home mortgages. Savings bonds differ from bonds in the sense that they are not guaranteed by the assets of a borrower. They are more like a ordinary bank term deposit.

Bonds are classed as a safe investment for investors, and they guarantee a regular return of interest to the holder. Further, they are cashable at full value (face value) at the time of their due date.

Bonds are issued by governments, municipalities, private companies and public organizations like hospitals, school boards and federal corporations. The value listed on a bond represents its face value, which is the amount the investor pays and is the amount returned to the investor at the due date.

Savings bonds sold by the government are of a different sort. They are in fact debentures as they are not guaranteed by the assets of the government. However they are a high quality investment because they are backed by the government and its powers of unlimited taxation. Savings bonds cannot be traded on the stock market but they can be sold back at face value to the government at any time.

Other types of bonds are traded on the stock market by brokers specializing in these types of investments. The price they are traded for however is not necessarily for their face value. Prices are established taking into account all the other investments available to investors. Let's look at how this goes.

In 1981 you bought a U.S. Government Bond of $1,000 titled U.S. 12.5%, Dec. 1994. This means that you hold a bond that pays you $125 interest a year just until 1994. At this time (due date) the government will reimburse you the $1,000 full value.

Suppose you want to sell this bond in 1987 when the current interest rate of new U.S. Bonds are around 10% per year. Here you will obtain a cash value more than $1,000 because your bond has an interest rate of 2.5% more than the current rate and this rate is good for another 7 years. The supply and demand factor comes into play and your bond price would go to $1,120. For a net yield (return) to a new buyer of 10% which is the same as the new U.S. Bond paying 10% interest.

Inversely, the sale of a similar bond having an interest rate of 7 or 8% would give to a holder a lesser cash value than the face value. This would be around $900 assuring the investor a net yield of 10% just to the due date.

Another factor to be aware of in setting the market value of bonds is the financial stability of the issuer. Even if his bonds are guaranteed by his assets there could always be a snag. For companies that issue bonds are not always in shape to regularly pay the interest due each year or even honor the cash face value at the due date.

Bonds reflect their market value by the various types of asset guarantees. They can be backed by first or second mortgages, guaranteed by security of company name only, face value reimbursable on fixed dates, etc. Each bond type corresponds to a different risk and the needs of particular investors.

14. Towards the Year 2001

Our investment portfolio celebrates its first year, so let's see what results we have (view table on next page). We see that we have earned $2,760 interest for a yield of 13.8% in one year. Not bad!

In flipping through the business pages we find an interesting investment. It's a bond with a face value of $1,000 but the current market price is just $932. Could it be a forgotten bargain?

After some examination we see that this Treasury Bond due on May 2001 has an interest rate of only 13.125% per year, while the current long term rate is at more than 14%. Also it does not allow any full reimbursement until the due date. This is why its price is not too high. But this current value offers all the same an annual interest rate of $131.25 and with an investment of $932 this gives a yield of 14.1% per year. Kind of interesting! Even more so since we anticipate an eventual let up on high credit rates soon to spur the economy. For if the interest rates fall, even mildly, the price of our bond will go up in reverse.

We make the decision and buy 12 individual bonds at $1,000 each of U.S. Treasury Bonds 13.125%, May 2001. If the future goes our way we will make our first capital gain next year. At the price of $932 each, we even have a little money left in our bank account. Since our Savings Bonds are paying 14% interest it is a good idea to keep them for now.

The net balance of our investments including the brokers commissions on our buys give us a portfolio market value of $22,424. A net appreciation of 12.1% in one year.

Transactions	**1982**				
Transactions	**Qty**		**Price**	**Total $**	**Cash $**
Cash: Bank deposit @ 13.6%					10,000
Interest: Bank deposit				1,360	11,360
Interest: U.S. Savings Bonds	10	@	140.00	1,400	12,760
Buy: U.S. Treasury Bonds 13.125% May 2001	12	@	932	11,520	1,240

Portfolio	**1982**			
Best value		**Qty**	**Cost $**	**Market value $**
U.S. Savings Bonds 14%		10	10,000	10,000
U.S. Treasury Bonds 13.125% May 2001		12	11,520	11,184
Cash: Bank deposit @ 14.5%			1,240	1,240
Sub-total			**22,760**	**22,424**
Total			**22,760**	**22,424**
Initial investment and % of variation since 1981			**20,000**	**12.1**

Recovery

15. Fiscal Policies

The principal role of governments is to increase the happiness of individuals and the various societies in the population that elects them. Whether they are municipal, provincial or federal governments, they try through all means to administer the resources of the nation in the best way. And to increase and equally share these resources amongst all citizens.

The federal government has certain exclusive tools at its hand. It controls the money supply, has large powers of taxation, and plays the role of leader amongst other government levels. The federal system determines the guidelines to follow in combatting negative effects of economic cycles. It tries to assure full employment (or almost) and tries to maintain maximum production growth, all without provoking excessive inflation.

We already know that monetary policy is one of the key ways it has to attain these objectives.

This is done by the Federal Reserve Bank setting the interest rate levels to control the money and credit supply of the nation. The other tool it has is the federal budget, which comprises the revenues and expenditures of the federal government. This Federal financial budget tool (more like monster) is called fiscal policy.

The mechanics of fiscal policy are relatively simple. In the course of making a budget, the state plans an impressive number of expenditures. A large part of this spending covers current traditional operations such as highways, recreation, education, health, defence, etc.

Another part is spent to stimulate economic regional and industrial sector development. Here the government invests directly or gives out loans and grants to certain economic areas where it wants to encourage growth. Or it makes its expenditures in selected regions in order to help create new plants and jobs.

Finally, another chunk of spending is used to combat the negative effect of economic cycles. For example, the state increases its spending considerably when private sector investments are weak or non-existent. Then when business and consumers re-launch their spending the state pulls back. The government also acts to smooth out the negative social impacts of recessions by paying (or increasing) unemployment and welfare benefits.

One sees the government then, through its financial expenditures, continually making adjustments to economic cycles.

Parallel to its spending policies, the government is also active in obtaining revenue, as it is necessary to finance its huge expenditures. Its principal source of revenue lies in corporate and personal income taxes.

During the 1930's the custom for government budgets was to balance their expenditures with their revenue. One can imagine the effect of such a deal. On one hand, the state injected money into the economy to stimulate it. And on the other hand it withdrew money through heavy taxation. In all, its actions amounted to zero for the economy. Now with the experience of past economic crises and budget theory refinement, the notion of government deficits has come into play.

The deficit is now perceived as a major tool of fiscal policy. When it is necessary to stimulate economic growth, the state spends money raising the deficit rather than increasing taxation. In expansionary periods the state reduces its expenditures. At the same time it profits from the natural flow of income tax revenue from the new labour force employed. It can also generate budget surpluses by applying tax increases towards the goal of cooling down the economy when necessary.

The deficit and surplus budget exercise gives us the notion of public debt. During a long economic cycle deficits and surpluses should theoretically cancel each other out. Deficits should grow during economic downturns and surpluses should in turn increase in economic upturns.

However in reality, they don't. Politicians rarely succeed in attaining this ideal balance, as they are always pressed by the unlimited needs of the population. And an eyeball on the next election! Thus we see a steady mushrooming of the public debt, at all government levels for that matter.

It should be highlighted that the massive public debts like that of the U.S. and Canada cause major economic and social problems. Both internal and external. A government, like a household or a private business, cannot continue to grow infinitely in debt to pay off its current bills. Sooner or later drastic measures must curb them.

16. The Stock Market

We have learned there exists a myriad of financial institutions. But we can confirm without a doubt that none of them enjoy the same prestige as the stock market. And yet the stock markets remain little known to the vast public.

The origin of the stock market arose from organized commercial exchanges for goods. With the need to negotiate letters of exchange for commercial goods, the market gradually developed into what we know today.

We want to tell you right away that the stock markets, although well regulated by governments, are not their institutions. They are non-profit organizations that assume the function of selling or buying shares of companies listed on the stock exchanges.

Their revenue comes from fees of stock (securities) brokers who in turn are members, and from these fees the Exchanges pay the costs of listing company shares on the markets. In the U.S. the most important exchanges are in New York, Chicago, and San Francisco. The principal Canadian stock exchanges are in Toronto, Montreal, and Vancouver. Elsewhere in the world the major exchanges are in London, Paris, Tokyo, Hong Kong, etc.

The stock market constitutes one of the most pure and dynamic applications of supply and demand. Imagine a little the function. At each moment, there are millions of investors ready to buy or sell shares. Investors forward their buy or sell orders to brokerage firms who are members of the stock exchanges. Here the brokers send these orders directly to their traders who work right on the floor of the exchange building.

In the case of the ordinary markets for goods and services that we know, there are numerous points of sale all over. Buyers never know at any time when is the best time to buy. Moreover, the products offered for sale differ greatly in their quality and quantity. This makes comparisons very difficult. Ordinary markets also have limited inventories of goods at any one place, and delivery delays are common. The mechanism of competition is far from perfect in the ordinary marketplace.

On the stock exchange all buyers and sellers are found in one market. Through electronic magic all buy and sell orders are made almost instantly and in the best competitive conditions. The product is simple, homogeneous, and there are no transport delays. Everything is confirmed immediately on the spot by a simple phone call to your broker.

An efficient market like this however, does create a marked sensitivity for outside events of all sorts. When a rumor sparks the slightest bad news, the stocks of all companies directly or indirectly involved risk falling under a rush of sell orders. And because time delays are short between an investor's decision and the execution of his order on the trading floor, there are not many buffers to soften the waves or cool out emotions.

One of the only brakes on panic movements are the brokers themselves, who are between the investors and traders. The brokers who are in the frontline of the game can act as personal advisors to their customers. They can soften any bad news and give customers a more neutral rundown of the events using their experience and access to additional information.

However this braking action is fading with the use of better electronic communications between the exchanges and customers. Also the growth of Discount Brokers is changing the game.

The discount brokers offer cheaper commissions on trades but do so without comment or advice. Their rapid increase in the market follows the general trends to standardisation and depersonalisation of all financial services. A prime example of this is the massive use of automatic bank teller machines today.

The moving trends of stocks on the markets are measured by indexes. Even though there exist several ways to calculate indexes, they are always the average of any trend of the stocks in certain groups.

The Dow-Jones is the most well known and one of the oldest around. However, it only represents the average moves of 30 companies' shares (blue chips) on the New York Exchange (called Wall Street). Its reputation stems from early American financial history and the fact that the companies listed on it are the largest and most powerful in the world (or almost). Other famous indexes are Standard & Poors, like the S & P 400, 100, etc. The S & P 500 represents the 500 largest companies on the New York Exchange.

Every Exchange has its own indexes which measure average share moves registered on it. The Toronto Exchange has 17 sector indexes: the TSE 300 (the largest 300 Canadian companies); the TSE 35 (most financially stable and traded) and others.

17. 1983 Recovery

At the end of 1983, the great economic gurus take the temperature of their patient. Inflation at a 3.9% increase. Not bad! But they don't make a hasty diagnosis and examine further. Gross National Product at a 3.6% increase. Return to the 1981 level. Personal consumption expenditures on goods and services at a 5.3% increase. Not bad at all! Private capital investments: no increase, even a slight decline. Perfect! It seems that business is remaining cautious.

One must not risk killing the patient while treating him. And there is no question of putting him back on his feet too soon. The experts continue the examination. New car sales are at 9,179,000 units. It was ten years ago that sales were at the same level.

However, housing construction increased 60.4% to 1,703,000 units started. Excellent! We have the right sector to gently push the economic relaunch. A durable good, very necessary and not luxurious (most of the time). Also house construction generates an economic impact throughout all sectors of the economy.

But there is a black mark on the wall: unemployment. The massive arrival of new workers has drowned the market. The civilian labor force has risen by 1.1 million new recruits that had waited on the sidelines during the recession. Consequently the unemployment rate kept to its high level of 9.6%. One must act on this. Especially since it is the young under the age of 25 that lack work who are the hardest hit.

A last glance at the Index of Industrial Production shows an increase of 5.9% which is fairly reasonable. One can now give a small stimulus to the economy and fix the banks' prime rate around 11%. This could start to cure the patient without endangering his life.

18. Stocks

When an economic recovery arrives then, the small to medium sized businesses immediately see good possibilities to develop and expand. They start to think of enlarging their operations, buying new production equipment, expanding their distribution networks and increasing their advertising and promotion.

Financing these investments can be done in several ways. The owner of a business can dig into his pocket for past profits but his investment needs generally exceed these funds. He can obtain a loan from the banks or other financial institutions specializing in loans to SMBs for expansion purposes. Or he can issue bonds or debentures on his company.

These financial instruments let the owner remain in total control of his business. But they also have some inconvenience. For rapid expansion of a business has a risk. Creditors insist on solid guarantees and a good return on their capital they invest. Even more, they impose on the borrower tough reimbursable conditions that he could have difficulty in meeting, if business slows or turns bad.

In the face of this, owners often prefer to sell a part of their stock ownership rights to partners. Here they all accept to share the risk equally. If business goes well, everybody wins. If it goes badly, everyone loses. Because share ownership contrary to bonds and bank type loans are not reimbursable to the buyers.

This partnership notion is called share participation through issuance. The business goes public by offering to individuals the right to buy a part of its assets. The buyer becomes a shareholder and actually owns a piece of the company. In this instance, one indirectly participates in the management of the business by naming directors of the company at every annual meeting. Enough theory then.

In practice, the owners-issuers of stock try to maintain, by all means, their control over their company. They keep a 50% or more block of stock or they assure that the shares in circulation are spread among a large number of holders. Knowing the little interest that the majority of people have in attending annual meetings, they can carry majority votes on all matters with as little as 20 to 30% share ownership.

Control of ownership can also be assured by other methods. The most popular share type issue is the common share. These common shares generally give a voting right to each holder. There equally exists privileged shares which do not give voting rights to holders. There are subordinating shares having an inferior voting right to common shares. Company directors issue for example subordinate shares with just one voting right per share and keep for themselves common shares with 10 voting rights each.

This practice then, permits the founders of a company or the directors to remain in control of the business and head off any takeover by an outside investor. This can be reassuring to new shareholders in knowing that the company will continue to be managed by the founders who usually have the best experience for the business.

The snag here is that this practice does not respect the democratic process of one vote per share. As long as power stays in the most competent shareholders' hands however, all goes well. But when these shareholders retire or sell their shares to others, the subordinate holders are not always assured of equal fair treatment.

There are other types of shares: participating, privileged with voting rights, reimbursable, cumulative dividends, convertible, variable rates, etc. Each again represents an investment type depending on the particular financial needs of a company. And the taste of risk for the investor. For one can guess that a share having inferior type voting rights to common shares will offer the holder special privileges somewhere along the line.

Moving along, how is the value of a share established on the market? Its price depends essentially on two factors. The capacity of the company to generate profits and investors' confidence it it.

For a share to be attractive on the market it must offer its buyer a yield hopefully superior to other investment vehicles. Why invest in shares when the market fluctuates so much. Especially when one can buy Savings Bonds with a guaranteed yield. For two reasons really.

One because of an eventual dividend that will offer a yield, even though lower than conservative investments. Two because there is always the possibility of a capital gain, which is an increase in the share's market value compared to its purchase price.

These two elements, dividends and capital gain, depend essentially on a company's profits. The company can decide to give some profits to its shareholders in the form of a dividend. This assures a regular revenue to the shareholder. Or the company can reinvest in its business which generates an increase in its net assets and in turn raises its market value.

However, this rule is not always applicable in the short or mid-term. For the stock market is one of confidence, hope and anticipation. Much more than actual profits are the future profits or loses of a company that determines the market price of shares. In order to emphasize this one can look at several financial ratios.

By dividing the market price of a share by its dollar profit we can obtain a price/earnings ratio. This ratio is the most popular one for evaluating shares. In certain cases it can hit 30, 50, or even 200, which gives the investor great confidence that the profits of this company will increase considerably over the future. In other cases, this ratio stays under 10 and sometimes slides to 4 or 5, reflecting a total lack of confidence in the future of these companies.

This simple ratio doesn't give us the exact financial situation of a company. For that, one must read the financial statements, consider its debt and its liquid assets, know the value of its management team, account for its competitive position and all other factors that can influence its actual and future profits.

But it is always necessary to remember that at any given time a stock trading on the market has no more value than what a buyer wants to pay for it. This conception of what investors have on the value of a stock determines the market price moves. When buyers fear a coming recession that will lower a companiy's profits, they sell their shares and put their capital in safe investments guaranteeing better yields. The gleam of an economic pickup produces the opposite effect, pushing the price/earnings ratios towards new highs.

All these decisions are often taken in an euphoric or panic mood which is characteristic of the stock market. And above all, the market reacts to anticipations, by always discounting what will happen. With all the chances of error this brings.

19. A Good Stock

1983 was a good year for our portfolio. Besides interest received on our savings account and bonds we have made a predicted capital gain. In effect, interest rates have dropped a little and our Treasury Bonds of 2001 have seen their price rise reflecting the current market rates. They have gone from $932 to $1152 for a annual yield of 11.4%. The total gain on capital reaches $2,300.

This success pushes us to look for other bargains. Maybe we should take a shot at the stock market? Besides is not the economy having a pickup? The hope of making new capital gains spurs us on. We decide to sell then, part of our Savings Bonds even with their high 14% yield.

But we remain conservative and buy 300 shares of Bankers Trust New York Corp. After all, do not banks represent one of the most solid financial institutions in the country?

These trades put our net capital at $28,017 for a total appreciation of 40% since 1981.

Transactions	**1983**			
Transactions	**Qty**	**Price**	**Total $**	**Cash $**
Cash: Bank deposit @ 14.5%				1,240
Interest: Bank deposit			180	1,420
Interest: U.S. Savings Bonds	10 @	140.00	1,400	2,820
Sell: U.S. Savings Bonds	5 @	1,000	5,000	7,820
Interest: U.S. Treasury Bonds 13.125% May 2001	12 @	131.25	1,575	9,395
Buy: Shares Bankers Trust New York Corp	300 @	22.44	6,934	2,461

Portfolio	**1983**		
Best value	**Qty**	**Cost $**	**Market value $**
U.S. Savings Bonds 14%	5	5,000	5,000
U.S. Treasury Bonds 13.125% May 2001	12	11,520	13,824
Cash: Bank deposit @ 9.1%		2,461	2,461
Sub-total		**18,981**	**21,285**
Superior value			
Shares: Bankers Trust New York Corp.	300	6,934	6,732
Sub-total		**6,934**	**6,732**
Total		**25,915**	**28,017**
Initial investment and % of variation since 1981		**20,000**	**40.1**

Expansion

20. Futures Contracts

And now let's play a little with the last key investment instrument, the futures contracts. But in advance, let's look at their mechanics through a simple example.

You own a business that fabricates aluminum counters. You maintain at all times an important inventory of the metal. Presently this poses no problem as the price of aluminum sheet is low. But in following the business news you realize that demand is rising rapidly and the price risks to rise in the future. What can you do to protect yourself from this predictable increase and guarantee a supply at the current price?

You guess that it is a good idea to buy a future contract. This will let you purchase the aluminum you need at a certain date at the present price. Of course, another person will contract (agree) to pay the difference between the current price and the future price when you make your purchase. And this person expects some compensation in return for the risk.

In a general way, a future is a contract between two parties. One, the seller, who accepts to take the calculated risk on the future value of a good, a stock, or commodity. And the other, the buyer, who prefers to pay immediately a premium in order to know for sure the price he will pay later. Between these two players there is a specialist broker who arranges the trade and assures its respect.

The premium fixed by the seller varies considerably with the risk he runs and with the particular situation. In the previous example, it could be that the seller really had a good aluminum inventory. Here he must make a judgment call on the future price of the metal. Is it better to accept the market price during the course of several months and hope that the price rises much later? Or run the risk of a decrease in price?

The trading of futures contracts, one sees, is not for amateurs. One has to know the futures market very well and be abreast of the moves of the economy. Also to predict panic moves and have the money to cover contracts at all times. Because of these factors, futures contracts primes vary rapidly daily and even hourly. The slightest good or bad news shoots the price upwards or downwards and even causes major market collapses.

Taken in a large sense, the futures most accessible to investors are stock warrants and stock options.

A warrant is a right to buy stock directly from a company at a given price over a certain period of time. Often this period is extended. The share is issued directly by the company and warrants are traded on the market like all shares. Its value depends on the conditions that can be exercised. Its market price will be all the more higher if one can buy the shares at a better price than the current price. Also if its life is long and the company in question has a good future.

Options have similar characteristics but their life does not last more than a year. There are buy (or call) options and sell (or put) options. They can be issued by any investors, and not only by companies carrying their name, as in the case of warrants.

A sell option called XYZ$22, June 1988 gives its holder the right to buy 100 shares of XYZ at $22 at anytime up to June 1988. A complex mechanism fixes all the details of this market; exercise dates, issuance, buys and sells, eligible shares, identification of the issuers who must respect the exercised options, etc.

It is important to note that futures play, above all, an important role in financial and economic planning. They let investors and producers downgrade their short to mid-term risks. It also lets them maximize the profit on their companies net worth. And accountants love this sort of thing.

In many cases, bold investors play this market for speculative gains. A typical example gives a buy right to another investor without owning the shares themselves. This means that during the life of the option the seller only promises to deliver to the buyer, on demand, the shares.

If the market price does not pass the exercise price, the seller pockets the premium quoted for his risk taken. If conversely, the actual share price rises, the buyer demands delivery of the shares. And he does this in order to resell them at a profit on the market.

In reality, a compensation mechanism generally avoids the real transaction on the shares in question. But it makes the seller pay an equivalent amount of money so the buyer can realize his profit.

21. 1984 Expansion

In 1984, the growth of the Gross National Product (GNP) wavered near 7%. Such an increase was not seen for more than ten years. And in spite of this growth, the CPI rose only 4.3%.

The strong GNP growth can be partly explained by personal consumer expenditures increase of 2.8%. The consumers were gradually regaining confidence in the future. New car sales rose strongly to 10,400,000 vehicles. Housing construction kept to its 1.7 million units level of 1983.

Fixed capital business investments rose only 1.1%. This indicated that actual production machinery and equipment was doing the trick at the moment. One will continue to use the capacity at hand: adding later. While waiting, the economy will not be pressed too much in its demands for new equipment.

Even unemployment started to fall off. The high rate reversed itself and slipped to 7.5% from 9.6%. The worst had passed. This improvement enabled 2.2 million new job seekers to join the active, looking for work, population. These job seekers were absorbed by the creation of 3.3 million jobs during the year.

With all this good news, it is useless to stimulate the economy by outside measures as it is re-establishing itself nicely. However it is necessary to maintain the banks' prime rate at a 11% level to avoid overheating the economy.

22. Diversification

We have seen in 1984 the government authorities feared relaunching the economy too rapidly. At the year's mid-point the interest rate rose slightly. The market value of our Bonds May 2001 fell to $991 each from $1152 a year earlier. Also our Bankers Trust shares which cost $6,934 slipped to $6,039 reflecting poorer profits than forecast.

This first minor reverse doesn't discourage us at all. On the contrary! The worry of the state containing inflation is comforting. The economic pickup will be strong and the following growth more stable.

We continue on with our market investments but this time, we will select stocks more sensitive to economic cycles. Bank stocks, in effect, often adopt an anti-cyclical behavior. Like other essential economic sectors of food products or public utilities. These stocks form a refuge during economic downturns. When growth returns their market prices, inversely, do not appreciate as much as the industrial stocks.

However, our choice is a wise one. We go for 200 common shares of Digital Equipment Corporation. D.E.C. is a progressive computer company and it will certainly follow an eventual market rise.

We also decide to buy 400 shares of Chrysler Corporation. This investment is a little bolder than the others so we place it in the Good Quality Value group, rather than that of the Superior Value. The company has recently undergone new top management and should soon return to profitability.

Our portfolio now displays a capital appreciation of 38.7%, a slight drop from last year.

Transactions	1984				
Transactions	**Qty**		**Price**	**Total $**	**Cash $**
Cash: Bank deposit @ 9.1%					2,461
Interest: Bank deposit				224	2,685
Interest: U.S. Treasury Bonds 13.125% May 2001	12	@	131.25	1,575	4,260
Dividends: Bankers Trust New York Corp.	300	@	1.13	339	4,599
Interest: U.S. Savings Bonds	5	@	140.00	700	5,299
Sell: U.S. Savings Bonds	5	@	1,000	5,000	10,299
Sell: U.S. Treasury Bonds 13.125% May 2001	4	@	991	3,845	14,144
Buy: Shares Digital Equipment Corp.	200	@	40.00	8,240	5,904
Buy: Shares Chrysler Corp.	400	@	10.90	4,492	1,413

Portfolio 1984			
Best value	**Qty**	**Cost $**	**Market value $**
U.S. Treasury Bonds 13.125% May 2001	8	7,680	7,928
Cash: Bank deposit @ 11.8%		1,413	1,413
Sub-total		**9,092**	**9,341**
Superior value			
Shares: Bankers Trust New York Corp.	300	6,934	6,039
Shares: Digital Equipment Corp.	200	8,240	8,000
Sub-total		**15,174**	**14,039**
Good quality value			
Shares: Chrysler Corp.	400	4,492	4,361
Sub-total		**4,492**	**4,361**
Total		**28,758**	**27,741**
Initial investment and % of variation since 1981		**20,000**	**38.7**

23. International Trade

Just to here, we have been talking about the nation's economic behavior in closed circuit. In reality, we know there are large trade exchanges between world nations. We will look a little at this scene on international trade and money movements.

International trade is based on the notion of regional specialisation resembling that of the domestic economy. Why, for example, does the auto industry concentrate in Michigan while the newsprint industry lies for the most part in the South?

In the first case, it is mainly because Michigan is close to steel and rubber plants. It is here that the North American auto industry was born and that the transport costs are cheaper to this state. The newsprint industry in the South is where the abundant natural forest resources are.

Besides these major factors there are many other reasons like political decisions, regional development, human initiative, water routes, etc. Often the original reasons for industrial concentration disappear with time. To this extent the phenomenon of traditional concentration risks melting away. Then again it could remain for many years due to new factors like the U.S./Canada free trade agreements.

The same reasons apply to international trade. U.S. uses its rich and vast natural resources to upgrade its exports on goods and materials. On the other hand, our imports contain mainly finished manufactured products.

The reverse situation applies to Japan. Having to import the majority of its raw materials, Japan has developed its talents to the maximum in manufacturing finished high quality products. This permits it to export huge quantities of these products throughout the world.

Each nation exports then its own special resources in order to import the goods it lacks. And as natural resources are rare, a country can also look to export its services rather than goods. This is the case for Switzerland who sells its financial services throughout the world, or the countries in the Sunbelt who sell their valuable climates to tourists.

All these trades are made with currency, that is foreign currency, because we must pay in the currency of several countries at the same time.

International trade is made in the currency of the seller. The purchase of a Japanese television must be paid in yen; a German car in deutschmarks; a vacation in Canada in Canadian dollars. The fact is that currencies are bought and sold like ordinary goods and are subject to the same laws of supply and demand.

Because of the U.S. importance in the modern world economy, the U.S. dollar is still the most used currency for reference to other nations currencies. The yen, franc and pound sterling, to the most exotic are compared daily to U.S. dollars. This means that the U.S. dollar is the universal currency that one accepts for international settlements, along with that of gold. This reflects (or did) the general confidence that nations have in the American economy.

The value of a currency depends above all else on the economic health of the nation that issues it.

Who would want to hide in his safe the currencies of banana republics with economies of dwarfs?

Who can assure a banker of the future value of these currencies and of their capacity to be accepted all the time for goods and services? As long as the U.S. dollar, the yen, and the deutschmark symbolize strong and productive economies the trading world has confidence in the future.

This notion of confidence explains the periodic fluctuations of exchange rates between currencies. It can be said that the relative values of currencies are set by the economic strength of the nations they represent. Take for example the U.S. and Japan.

Goods made in Japan have been gradually acquired by the world over the last 25 years. They have a high quality value. The costs of producing these goods is relatively little as the Japanese workers are very efficient. Their salaries rise slowly. All nations buy Japanese cars, electronics, ships, trains, and even computers. In order to pay for their purchases the world needs yen that is constantly appreciating with this great demand.

In regards to the U.S. however, the situation is deteriorating. U.S. products don't have the reputation anymore that once made it the envy of the world. Production costs inflate constantly under the pressure of high salaries and decreasing hours of work. The world demand for American goods and services is slowing down, along with a lesser demand for U.S. currency that is weakening all the time.

In summary, the currency game generates a constant adjustment between the economies of countries. When the U.S. dollar loses its face value to the yen, Japanese products become more expensive for Americans. Inversely, American products become more accessible to the Japanese.

Multiply this example by more than 100 countries. Add the psychological factors, the speculator's moves in currencies, the particular economic ties between certain nations, the excessive reactions of financial wizards, the movements of international capital, the socialist economies, the particular situations of nations inflation and budget deficits, the discount rate variations ... And we see the daily market fluctuations of foreign currencies.

But above all of these factors, one must remember that the mid to long term value of a currency depends upon the economic health of a country. And this stems from the quality of its population, its ingenuity, its energetic workforce and its capacity to adjust to the lifestyle at the moment.

24. The Economy in 1985-1986

The 1985-1986 period was one of typical controlled economic expansion. The GNP rose respectively 3% and 2.9%, while inflation continued to slow at 3.2% and 2.6%.

The banks prime rate was borne along by regular drops just to 7.5% at the end of 1986, due to not having much pressure from lenders on it. This rate was now considered quite acceptable by most people.

Mortgage rates ceased to be considered a prohibitive luxury and they launched housing construction to 1.7 and 1.8 million units in the period. Concerning the actual slow demographic situation of the country at this time, these numbers represented a very strong activity.

New car sales broke all time records and hit over 11 million each year. The value of retail sales jumped 4.9% in 1985 and 5.3% in 1986. Businesses increased their fixed capital investments by 7.9% in 1985 and 6.2% in 1986 due to rising demands of consumers and reasonable financial interest rates.

The weather outlook was sunny. Salary increases remained modest and hours of work increased. Workers and their unions were not yet free of the recession. The unemployment rate continued to improve, falling to 7% in 1986 for the first time in 7 years.

Businessmen, on their side, held up their expansion and limited their profit growth to 4.6% in 1985 and -0.8% in 1986. In spite of this modest performance, the Index for Market Prices of In dustrial Shares appreciated by more than 45% in the two years. The good years were coming again and the financiers were ready.

25. A Little Boldness

In 1985, our portfolio posted a very encouraging performance. Economic expansion made a positive mark on each of our investments.

The bank discount rate decline had an immediate effect on all interest rates in the country. Our Treasury Bonds hit a high of $1,172 each for a capital gain of more than 25% from our purchase at $932. Thus, we profit by this opportunity and sell 4 coupons to obtain new cash for other market investments.

Concerning our stocks, almost all our shares are increasing rapidly. Besides the dividends that are accumulating, we see capital gains of 58% on Bankers Trust and 42% on Chrysler. Our Digital Equipment is growing slower but it also shows a gain of nearly 13% over one year.

These handsome results convince us to hang in with these market investments. We even decide to enlarge our portfolio with a stock on the lower end of our Good Value group, Merrill Lynch & Co. Inc. This large securities broker is very active in trading retail stocks. The stock should profit greatly with the expected securities business announced over the next few years.

Our portfolio has run for 4 years now. Starting with $20,000 in capital it is now valued at $38,801, a total appreciation of 94%.

Transactions	1985				
Transactions	**Qty**		**Price**	**Total $**	**Cash $**
Cash: Bank deposit @ 11.8%					1,413
Interest: Bank deposit				167	1,579
Interest: U.S. Treasury Bonds 13.125% May 2001	8	@	131.25	1,050	2,629
Dividends: Bankers Trust New York Corp.	300	@	1.23	369	2,998
Dividends: Digital Equipment Corp.	200	@	0.00	0	2,998
Dividends: Chrysler Corp.	400	@	0.27	107	3,105
Sell: U.S. Treasury Bonds 13.125% May 2001	4	@	1172	4,547	7,652
Buy: Shares Merrill Lynch & Co. Inc.	200	@	30.50	6,283	1,369

Portfolio	1985		
Best value	**Qty**	**Cost $**	**Market value $**
U.S. Treasury Bonds 13.125% May 2001	4	3,840	4,688
Cash: Bank deposit @ 7.6%		1,369	1,369
Sub-total		**5,209**	**6,057**
Superior value			
Shares: Bankers Trust New York Corp.	300	6,934	10,950
Shares: Digital Equipment Corp.	200	8,240	9,300
Sub-total		**15,174**	**20,250**
Good quality value			
Shares: Chrysler Corp.	400	4,492	6,394
Shares: Merrill Lynch & Co. Inc.	200	6,283	6,100
Sub-total		**10,775**	**12,494**
Total		**31,158**	**38,801**
Initial investment and % of variation since 1981		**20,000**	**94.0**

26. The Portfolio Explodes

Already 1986! One has little to say as the economy is running very well. The expansion continues to carry our portfolio towards an incredible high of $54,710. The total gain since 1981 has attained 174%. Could one hope for better results?

Let's take a glance at the source of these gains. All the items in our portfolio are doing well. The value of our Superior Value Shares has doubled in less than 3 years. Same result for our Chrysler Corp. shares classed in the Good Quality Value group.We took a bit of a gamble and we are well compensated for it. The prices of our shares have increased by almost 122%. Only our Merrill Lynch shares have risen slowly, yet have appreciated by 7% nevertheless. Now is the time to go all out and invest in a real speculative stock.

Our business readings tell us to go with Mattel Inc. The company is one of the largest independant manufacturers and marketers of toys in the world. The creators of Barbie dolls and Hot Wheels vehicles. The company doesn't lack new ideas in offering young America their playthings in this period of economic prosperity.

Also we go for 500 shares of Prime Computer Inc. This company is in computers and will surely follow the same path as Apple Computer. Pushing our share value into unknown horizons.

To finance these purchases, we sell our 4 Treasury Bonds that are our most safe but not the fastest growing investment in our portfolio. Their price now is more than their face value and we get $1,402 each for them.

In order to profit to the maximum in this boom period, we open a margin account with our broker to increase our investment opportunities. This account lets the stock buyer acquire stocks without paying the full cost for them. Brokers will accept to finance a portion of the value of stocks bought by an investor under certain financial conditions. The credit generally covers up to 50% of the stocks' value.

It must be understood that this type of financing centers on the market value of the stock and not on its purchase price. For example, when you buy a share for $20, you immediately pay $10 and go into debt for $10 with your brokerage firm. But at any time, this debt can not be any more than half the value of the share's market price.

If the share's price falls to $12, the credit of the broker goes to $6, or 50% of the market value. You must then reimburse a difference of $4 between your original debt of $10 and the allowed credit of $6.

This factor demanding reimbursement of a part of your credit is called a **margin call** and it is demanded immediately. If you cannot cover the amount owed, your broker will sell the guaranteed shares he holds. And you suffer the loss.

If conversely, the price of your share climbs to $30, your credit limit rises to $15.Thus, you can obtain a $5 extra credit from your broker.

We will be content on a first go with a margin of a mere $8,000 dollars. This will give us time to familiarize ourselves with this financing technique and to examine other market opportunities.

Transactions	1986					
Transactions	**Qty**		**Price**	**Total $**	**Cash $**
Cash: Bank deposit @ 7.6%					1,369
Interest: Bank deposit				104	1,473
Interest: U.S. Treasury Bonds 13.125% May 2001	4	@	131.25	525	1,998
Dividends: Bankers Trust New York Corp.	300	@	1.35	405	2,403
Dividends: Digital Equipment Corp.	200	@	0.00	0	2,403
Dividends: Chrysler Corp.	400	@	0.44	176	2,579
Dividends: Merrill Lynch & Co. Inc.	200	@	0.80	160	2,739
Sell: U.S. Treasury Bonds 13.125% May 2001	4	@	1,402	5,440	8,179
Buy: Shares Mattel Inc.	500	@	13.87	7,143	1,036
Buy: Shares Prime Computer Inc.	500	@	17.75	9,141	-8,105

Portfolio 1986			
	Qty	**Cost $**	**Market value $**
Best value			
Margin (7.75%)		-8,105	-8,105
Sub-total		**-8,105**	**-8,105**
Superior value			
Shares: Bankers Trust New York Corp.	300	6,934	14,700
Shares: Digital Equipment Corp.	200	8,240	15,600
Sub-total		**15,174**	**30,300**
Good quality value			
Shares: Chrysler Corp.	400	4,492	9,955
Shares: Merrill Lynch & Co. Inc.	200	6,283	6,750
Shares: Mattel Inc.	500	7,143	6,935
Sub-total		**17,918**	**23,640**
Speculative value			
Shares: Prime Computer Inc.	500	9,141	8,875
Sub-total		**9,141**	**8,875**
Total		**34,128**	**54,710**
Initial investment and % of variation since 1981		**20,000**	**173.6**

Future and Uncertainty

27. Predict and Forecast

In launching this last chapter, let's go back to the business media. These people play a multiple role for their audience. The first is to report the facts, describe events, report on reality. Present results, numbers, data. The reporters succeed admirably in this task without confusing reality. After all, a fact is a fact!

However, the business and financial commentators - for those who listen - rapidly fall into a myriad of detail often quite banal. To this extent, they add their own personal analysis or that of others to the question of the day, trying to fatten the news through more body. Already starting to stretch the objective information to profit on their opinions. And that is not all.

Once facts are reported and analyses made, there is always the question of what this may hold for the future. The astrologists understood this quest of humanity at an early stage: trying to know what tomorrow brings. And they have profited from it since day one.

The economic and financial sectors have not escaped this question. Responses come from all areas: business journalists; private and public research centers; financial investment advisors; economists; politicians; professional investors; and the guy on the street. Everybody gets into the act, either good or bad.

Let's think seriously about this question. Has there ever been a major economic, political or social event that has been forecasted in advance with accuracy? A war? An economic crisis? A crash? Never!

This thought leads us to make a distinction between two notions then, forecasts and predictions.

Forecasts belong to the economists. An economic forecast can be presented in two ways. One way is in the form of a general announcement like *the present economic expansion will probably be followed by a period of slowdown or recession more or less intense, assuming that.....* Also one hears that the sun doesn't shine forever and sooner or later the rains will come. It is difficult to make a financial decision, even the slightest one, on this type of prose.

The second form of economic forecast is to the point *the economic growth of the U.S. economy in 1988 will be near 2.8%.* This firm declaration stems obviously from several hundred pages of hypotheses that are to the letter in detail. Ridiculous? Not at all!

In reality, this form of forecast recognizes clearly the great complexity of economic reality and the impossibility to forecast the future precisely. One must know that the future depends on a series of natural events and/or political decisions. Even the authorities who must make decisions cannot say in advance what will really happen.

When someone launches a forecast without using solid economic logic and without considering realistic hypotheses, we say they are predicting rather than forecasting. In fact they are expressing a wish rather than a sure and reasoned judgment of the future.

Must we qualify and correct these statements? No! The politician who predicts that the economy will certainly be better next year does in fact reply to the needs of assurance in the future. He tries to maintain and increase confidence which is the essential element of a healthy economy. And the broker who states that the markets are going to rise. Isn't he playing the same role for his customers ?

In summary, the instigators of predictions only express their own personal opinions. Or due to constant pestering of questions for which they don't have answers, they finally surrender to what the the audience only wants to hear. And everyone is reassured and satisfied.

28. Euphoria

In June 1987, the status of our portfolio has changed greatly from that of last year. We have gained more than $25,000. What should we do now? Wait? Sell?

We see no reason to sell any of our stocks. The economy is in excellent health. Inflation is under control and interest rates are not hindering expansion.

Of course, certain stocks appear to be peaking. In many cases they have appreciated from 300 to 500% in less than 24 months. It is the new companies that are attractive now, the ones in high technology and glamorous services. Last year, we went for Prime Computer and it gave us a 41% capital gain within one year. So we go for another high-tech winner this year.

Our choice is N.B.I. Inc. For computers are the future and what a value here. The stock will not stay at $12.25 a share for very long. We go for a big bang at 2,000 shares.

Next, to give more glamor to our portfolio we buy 10 option contracts ***Call GM Dec $70*** at $1475 each. One contract gives the the right to buy 100 shares of General Motors until December 1987 at $70. The market price is $83 per share now. Over the year it should hit paydirt with the way the market is rising these days. The effect on options in a rising market can push them 2 to 3 times their price with only a 20% increase in the common share.

We will finance a part of these buys from the sale of our Bankers Trust shares. We will cover the rest with recent credit increases on our margin account. There is nothing to do but sit back and wait for our profits. When is the first $100,000?

Transactions		**June 1987**		
Transactions	**Qty**	**Price**	**Total $**	**Cash $**
Margin (7.75%)				-8,105
Interest: Paid on margin			628	-8,733
Dividends: Bankers Trust New York Corp.	300 @	1.58	474	-8,259
Dividends: Digital Equipment Corp.	200 @	0.00	0	-8,259
Dividends: Chrysler Corp.	400 @	0.74	296	-7,963
Dividends: Merrill Lynch & Co. Inc.	200 @	0.80	160	-7,803
Sell: Bankers Trust New York Inc.	300 @	54.50	15,860	8,056
Buy: Shares N.B.I. Inc.	2,000 @	12.25	25,235	-17,179
Buy: Options Call GM Dec $70	10 @	1475	15,193	-32,371

Portfolio	**June 1987**		
Best value	**Qty**	**Cost $**	**Market value $**
Margin (8.25%)		-32,371	-32,371
Sub-total		**-32,371**	**-32,371**
Superior value			
Shares: Digital Equipment Corp.	200	8,240	33,600
Sub-total		**8,240**	**33,600**
Good quality value			
Shares: Chrysler Corp.	400	4,492	14,000
Shares: Merrill Lynch & Co. Inc.	200	6,283	7,226
Shares: Mattel Inc.	500	7,143	5,315
Sub-total		**17,918**	**26,541**
Speculative value			
Shares: Prime Computer Inc.	500	9,141	12,940
Shares: N.B.I. Inc.	2,000	25,235	24,500
Option contracts Call GM Dec $70	10	15,193	14,750
Sub-total		**49,569**	**52,190**
Total		**43,355**	**79,960**
Initial investment and % of variation since 1981		**20,000**	**299.8**

29. Crash Economy

Since we mentioned that market moves depend on actual economic cycles, let's look at the world economic situation around the crash period.

An ideal scenario would find the world industrial nations in a bad state, close to major crises. However the actual situation was not like this at all.

The key indicator, inflation, is showing no sign of rising. The CPI rate runs at a 2% increase in the U.S. and a 4% increase in Canada while approaching zero in Germany and Japan. But then, could these 4 economies again be in recession? Let's look a little.

The unemployment rate is not moving up. In fact it is staying relatively stable. The bank discount rate is low enough to push more expansion and yet keep credit from exploding. In all, the GNP's of the 3 largest economies are running at 5 to 8% in real terms. One cannot find any negative signals here.

In flipping our business pages a little, we discover some anomalies. Two in particular. And they both touch the U.S..

The first concerns the American commercial trade deficit. The U.S. exports are stagnating around $210 billion since 1980. Inversely, the imports to the U.S. went from $250 to $400 billion in the same period. This generated a monthly deficit of around $15 billion. And this deficit is bleeding U.S. currency from within to the exterior. It has to buy a lot of yen, deutschmarks, and others to pay for these imports. In a nutshell, the country is going into hock with its trading partners.

But that is not all. There is another deficit problem with the federal budget. This is hitting close to $200 billion a year, and being financed by the U.S. dollars that Japan, Germany and others have from their big trade surpluses Here the mass amounts of U.S. dollars return in the form of purchases on bonds, stocks, real estate, businesses, and of course U.S. treasury bills. In brief, foreigners are buying up the American economy and paying for it with extravagant foreign purchases.

However we know in periods of economic expansion that sound management suggests reducing budget deficits - by increasing taxes or decreasing spending. But the President and Congress for various reasons, mainly political, have preferred to live with debt just to the absolute limit.

But this limit is fast approaching. The U.S. dollar being spent without counting is becoming an object of decreasing value. Having traded at 200 to 250 yen per dollar over the last ten years, the U.S. dollar is now at the 125 yen-level and going lower. It is falling against other strong foreign currencies also. The law of supply and demand is not always nice.

Thus, we have the key to the market crash. We can summarize it by emphasizing:

1. The world economy in general and the North American economy in particular has witnessed a controlled period of expansion since 1984. This gave strong confidence to stock market investors. Profits were high and brokers were ecstatic.

2. The U.S. trade deficit spewed dollars to the outside world. A large part of these dollars returned to help finance the enormous U.S. federal budget deficit.

3. Another chunk of U.S. dollars held by foreigners was placed in the stock markets in New York (mainly) but also in London, Toronto, etc. This constant fresh capital pushed up the markets to record highs.

4. From month to month the exchanges' indexes rose to new summits. We saw in the first half of 1987 the move of the pendulum to the positive side. Stock prices pushed up in great fury, looking for even greater profits.

5. With the growing chronic U.S. deficits, experts started to realize that the U.S. administration must act soon to stop this hemorrhaging. The more time passes the harder the fall. A law was passed by Congress gradually limiting the budget to fixed levels. And the trade gap cannot grow forever. It remains to be seen as to what will happen.

6. To reduce the deficit one must increase taxes or decrease expenditures. In both cases this gives consumers less money and decreases buying domestically and abroad. To this extent, Congress started talking of trade protectionism in order to reduce imports.

7. Some investors became scared about the U.S. reacting too quickly and wanted to know what would happen? The only answer was a world economic crisis! And with it: high interest rates; slow world trade; massive unemployment; and falling profits. The pendulum would reverse its swing.

8. The rest is routine. From a maximum of 2,722 points at mid-year the Dow-Jones Index started to slip down at a frightening pace. It had a few rebounds in September and early October. An increase in U.S. interest rates gave the money markets (Treasury Bonds, Corporate Bonds, etc.) a push up but the stock markets a slap. The trade deficit was out of control and drastic measures were needed. On October 19th the pressure hit its maximum level. Fear became panic and the reaction exaggerated, and we had the Crash!

9. Finally, a last word on the galloping rate of the stock market plunge. This partly stemmed from two new phenomena. Firstly because of extreme capital fluidity all around with the development of new international exchanges. Here, the entire world became an immense and unique financial market. Open at day in New York, the night in Tokyo and London, and inversely. Capital raced around at the speed of light. In a few hours (or less), billions of dollars jumped from treasury bills and bonds to stocks, then reversed itself as interest rates changed.

The second phenomenon that magnifies these financial moves was that of the famous program trading. Here, a larger and larger chunk of stocks, futures and options trading were being done by pre-programmed computers. Wall Street whiz kids were playing with automatic sell and buy orders when certain price conditions hit the market.By the time the authorities could stop this, it was too late!

30. The Crash Economy - In Debt Terms

What a great party then. Investors became rich in the stock market. And the U. S. consumed everything like crazy, created millions of jobs and produced war machines by the thousands. And it was done all at the same time, painlessly. Or so it appeared.

The dream of boom and power was flattened by the crash. Now the U.S. is being presented with the bill on its spending spree. Slowly yet surely put on the table by its foreign creditors, the Europeans and of course, Japan. And the tab comes to $400 billion at the moment, and is growing rapidly.

If the U.S. does not wind down the party soon, its foreign debt could hit a massive $1 trillion by the early 1990's . This is an IOU that will cut a large chunk out of the standard of living as we know it today.

Americans are not used to being in hock to other nations. For it is third world countries like Argentina or Brazil, or declining powers like Britain, that are strapped by debt. The U.S. has not been a debtor nation since 1914. It cannot understand the economic and social problems it presents and the loss of national sovereignty that follows.

The phenomenon of debt tells the story as the amount increases incessantly upwards. For in a few short years the U.S. has spent over 75 years of capital investments made abroad. Going from the world's biggest overseas creditor nation to its largest debtor. As recently as 1983 its investments abroad - stocks, bonds, real estate, factories - exceeded foreign investments in the U.S. by over $100 billion.

In a surprising reversal, two years later it was as if its tenants had become its landlords. Foreign assets in the U.S. surpassed its assets abroad by $112 billion. It is said that by the time a new President enters office in January 1989 foreign assets will rise by $500 to $600 billion. In effect, the U.S. will owe $500 to $600 billion more than they owe us. This rate of increase is incredible.

Even through simple arithmetic compounding, the U.S. is dropping more and more into debt. For as its foreign debt mounts, so do the net payments for the use of foreign capital. In 1986, it paid abroad a net $10 billion in interest, dividends, and rent. In 1987 it will be around $17 billion. Next year it will be $27 billion. By 1989 it could hit $40 billion. And in 1990 it could push to $50 billion to the Japanese, Germans, British, French and other foreign creditors.

These numbers may even be a pessimistic scenario. For a declining dollar can set a debt trap. Here the weak dollar allows foreign investors to buy into the U.S. at cheap prices. Less and lesser valued yen and marks are buying more and more stocks, bonds, real estate, and plants. The return on these investments - the dividends, rents, and profits - end up in foreign owned bank accounts. When the money is shipped abroad it puts further downward pressure on the U.S. dollar, making it yet cheaper for foreign investors to buy into the U.S. If then, the U.S. gets caught in this trap, it will be selling off an increasing piece of the nation at lower and lower prices.

But what about exports? With the dollar down almost 50% against the mark and the yen in just two years, U.S. products are selling fairly well overseas. Exports are up a little over 1986, and the trade deficit is slowly getting better. That's the problem: slowly. Exports are up but so are imports. America is still in love with foreign goods, buying a lot more than it produces at home. Even more than it can afford.

Although the trade deficit is improving, the current-accounts balance, which also includes financial flows of all types, is not doing well. A $25 billion reduction in the trade deficit in each of the next three years, if possible, will be mostly offset by increased payments on foreign debt - mainly interest and dividends. These payments could keep the current accounts deep in deficit, pushing overall debt toward the $1 trillion level in the 90's.

Every time the U.S. Treasury holds an auction to borrow money, one key question arises: What are the Japanese going to do? How much does the U.S. have to offer in interest to get them to buy the nation's bonds? Any mumble that the Japanese are not happy with current levels flares an immediate jump in interest rates.

The decline then, of the U.S. into debtor status may retain the growth of its exports even if the U.S. dollar continues to fall. For it is increasingly difficult for Washington to push Japan to open its economy up to U.S. imports while it holds out its hands to Tokyo at each monthly Treasury bond auction. You do not pressure your banker, especially if he is also your landlord and even employer.

Thus, American consumers were protected from the effects of going into global debt as long as the Japanese and Europeans were willing to hold and add to their financial assets the U.S. loans, mostly Treasury bonds, but also stock in U.S.

companies. The U.S. could consume more than it produced and spend more than it took in as taxes.

31. The Meltdown

During the morning of October 19th, the news bulletins were already talking of the market crash. Why be alarmed? Surely a few investors remembered the panic in 1929?

At noon, the news was confirmed. All the markets were melting. The lines to every broker were tied up. One watched and waited until the end of the day.

The next morning we took our reading. In less than 4 months our portfolio cascaded 49% going from $79,960 to $40,349.

Nothing to say! Nothing to do! It is too late to react.

Transactions	**Oct 19 1987**				
Transactions		**Qty**	**Price**	**Total $**	**Cash $**
None					

Portfolio	**Oct 19 1987**		
Best value	**Qty**	**Cost $**	**Market value $**
Margin (8.25%)		-32,371	-32,371
Sub-total		**-32,371**	**-32,371**
Superior value			
Shares: Digital Equipment Corp.	200	8,240	26,000
Sub-total		**8,240**	**26,000**
Good quality value			
Shares: Chrysler Corp.	400	4,492	10,800
Shares: Merrill Lynch & Co. Inc.	200	6,283	4,850
Shares: Mattel Inc.	500	7,143	4,625
Sub-total		**17,918**	**20,275**
Speculative value			
Shares: Prime Computer Inc.	500	9,141	8,935
Shares: N.B.I. Inc.	2,000	25,235	13,760
Option contracts Call GM Dec $70	10	15,193	3,750
Sub-total		**49,569**	**26,445**
Total		**43,355**	**40,349**
Initial investment and % of variation since 1981		**20,000**	**101.7**

32. Day After

Black Monday - October 19 - is already famous as the darkest day in Wall Street history. With good reason as the record 508 points plunge in the Dow Jones industrial average highlights a disaster that wiped out $500 billion in shareholder assets. However, the very next day, the Dow posted a record 102 points gain.

So within 24 hours, everything was suddenly upbeat then, right? Wrong! The market came closer to total meltdown the day after the crash than it had on Black Monday. Terrible Tuesday, newspapers dubbed it, that critical day. Some say that October 20 was the most dangerous day we had in 50 years. The fact we did not have a total meltdown does not mean we didn't have a breakdown.

Terrible Tuesday began with traders in a state of despair and got worse. Banks that normally lend heavily to security dealers had stopped doing so. Some demanded repayment of major loans that very day. This put a number of brokerage firms extremely close to financial bankruptcy.

The critical point came at mid-day: trading in stocks, options and futures in a variety of markets virtually braked to a stop. Many of the Blue Chip stocks on the Dow industrial average, including the most powerful IBM, could not be traded because there were simply no buyers for them. Major New York based investment and banking firms urged the chairman of the New York Stock Exchange to close the exchange to allow the market time to recover. But the chairman refused. As he said that if we had shut down the exchange, we would have never opened it again.

Decisive action by American regulatory and major investment banks halted the market's down spiral and apparently stopped a catastrophe. First, the Federal Reserve pumped several millions of dollars into the banking system. This was a marked signal to nervous trading that the U.S. Government was set on averting a market collapse. It was said that the president of the Federal Reserve Bank of New York had urged many top bankers to provide credit to stock brokers.

The crucial point, however, was probably a wild upward movement in the unfamiliar stock index, the future contract, traded on the Chicago Board of Trade. Here, buying or selling such a contract amounts to a gamble on which way the market will be going. In this instance, the bet was based on the Major Market Index (MMI), a category of blue-chip stocks similar to the Dow Jones average. In a five-minute span after 12:30 p.m. on Terrible Tuesday, the MMI futures had their most massive upswing in their history.

A group of major investment brokers made a concentrated and perhaps desperate effort to buy up MMI futures and reverse the market. As futures are purchased largely on credit, buyers were apparently able to place enough money into the contracts to produce a substantial swing in their price. News of this Chicago rally rapidly spread to New York, helping fire up the booming revival on NYSE.

Thus, in short, it was a very close call. But the near disaster on Terrible Tuesday, the day after the Crash, raises the specter that *such a crisis could strike again some day*.

The most worrisome thing is that the stock market crashed on that Monday and rose again on Tuesday without any major critical political or economic event pulling the trigger. Should a war, political assassination or other crisis of severe proportions strike, nobody actually can say just what it could do to the world's nervous stock markets again.

33. Conclusions

Time for a cursory wrap-up now. What is the future of the economy and the stock markets? What should the smaller investor do with his investments? Before replying, let's summarize what we have lived through.

We first spoke about a few economic laws that control our economic and financial activities. We tried to do so in a simplistic fashion by highlighting the institutions and investment instruments available.

Our goal was to inform and divert you a little. But we have also tried to stimulate you on the subject of economics as one of the more necessary and practical disciplines. After all, don't we continually live in a supply and demand situation? Is it not worth spending a little time trying to better understand what inexhaustible wants and scarce resources are all about?

We have stated that stock market cycles run with the fundamental and repetitive economic cycles. In order to show this, we have walked through the recent actual economic cycles. A high pressure period, recession, recovery, expansion and today's questionable period.

We finally looked at international trade and currency exchange problems.

And now we are going to make an economic prediction on the future. We will play economist and forecast on conservative hypotheses.

The general economic situation of the industrial nations is still healthy. This is supported by favorable economic indicators. Thus the probability of a marked recession in the short term is dubious.

Does this signify that the stock markets will return to their recent upswings? No way! The markets react to anticipation in strong periods of optimism. Today, investors are predicting and even wishing for a recession. And they don't even know why.

Will we relive another recession? In 1989? In 1990? The key is the U.S. If we don't find a solution to our problems of trade deficits and budget deficits or if we react too quickly, the answer is yes. The chances for a recession in the mid-term will accelerate and the markets will continue their slide.

If on the other hand the U.S. is aided by its trade partners, and gets its budget act together between Congress and the Executive Office we can escape a recession.

The markets could gain confidence again as investors go for future profits. But all investors must be reassured by meaningful U.S. action.

What can we conclude? This. In the mid and long term the market movements follow economic cycles. But in the short term the anticipation game makes for extreme uncertainty. Plus, the fluid international capital moves create giant waves of ups and downs on financial investments worldwide.

The stock and money markets will be hit more and more with these massive cash inflows and outflows and they will resemble lotteries rather than serious financial institutions.

How can a modest investor survive this circus? The only answer is the adoption of a cautious and flexible investment strategy.

This strategy can be summarized in 5 simple points

1. Inform yourself before acting. This does not only mean obtaining advice from friends and colleagues, or from your financial advisor. But to understand at least broadly, and on your own, the functioning of the investment instruments you favour. While doing this put your money in the banks and savings bonds.

2. Lose your illusions. One rarely becomes rich on market investments. These rather serve to manage your assets (already acquired through work) with the pace of economic growth. The hopes of rapid and spectacular gains hide dangerous traps.

3. Learn to limit ambitions. No one can predict with accuracy the turning points in the markets. Not even multimillionaires and their expert advisors. It is useless to play your chances to the limit. It is much better to get out six months before the end of a peak than the day after a crash.

4. Spread your assets. The best of investments should never get all the money. A balanced portfolio assures a riskless yield adequate for all periods of the economy.

5. Be patient. Patience is the great virtue of investors. One should never make investments unless one has lots of time to ride them out.

34. Final Balance

A month exactly after the crash, on November 19th, we prepare the final balance sheet on our investments.

Over the past few weeks margin calls have forced us to liquidate almost all our stocks. We stay with only two Good Value shares, Digital Equipment Corp. and Chrysler Corp. that guarantee our credit margin of $8,348.

Over the course of the last four months, since the end of June 1987, our portfolio's value has decreased from $79,960 to $27,402. A drop of 66%! How does one explain a fall as dramatic as this when during the same period the Dow-Jones index fell only 32%?

Part of the explanation lies in the fact that we did not have any of the 30 representative stocks (Blue Chips) that make up this famous index. The stocks in our portfolio were much less conservative and financially solid than the Blue Chips. And were thus more sensitive to panic that sweeps the stock markets.

But the principal reason is that our investment strategy was a sporadic one mainly concentrated over the last year of hectic activity. We willingly adopted the profile that characterizes most of the smaller investors on the eve of a market crash.

We ignored the advice of financial experts who had affirmed over several months that the markets were overvalued. We refused to cash in our profits of Good Quality Value and preferred to borrow large sums of money to buy more speculative stocks.

In sum, we had fallen into what they call **Market euphoria**. Easy gains leading to more and never ending profits. Thinking that nothing will stop the profit spiral.

But economic logic never tolerates one's movement too far away from it. In the end, the laws of scarcity and abundance always come back into play.

What is the result of our greed? The bottom line of our portfolio is $27,402. a gain of 37% over a period of 6 years. Was it really worth it?

Transactions	**Nov 1987**			
Transactions	**Qty**	**Price**	**Total $**	**Cash $**
Margin (8.25%)				-32,371
Interest: Paid on margin			1,113	-33,484
Sell: Shares Mattel Inc.	500 @	8.25	4,001	-29,483
Sell: Shares Prime Computer Inc.	500 @	14.63	7,096	-22,387
Sell: Shares N.B.I. Inc.	2,000 @	4.75	9,215	-13,172
Sell: Options Call GM Dec $70	10 @	50.00	485	-12,687
Sell: Shares Merril Lynch & Co. Inc.	200 @	22.37	4,340	-8,348

Portfolio	**Nov 1987**		
	Qty	**Cost $**	**Market value $**
Best value			
Margin (7.75%)		-8,348	-8,348
Sub-total		**-8,348**	**-8,348**
Superior value			
Shares: Digital Equipment Corp.	200	8,240	26,250
Sub-total		**8,240**	**26,250**
Good quality value			
Shares: Chrysler Corp.	400	4,492	9,500
Sub-total		**4,492**	**9,500**
Speculative value			
Sub-total		**0**	**0**
Total		**4,384**	**27,402**
Initial investment and % of variation since 1981		**20,000**	**37.0**

Definitions

ACQUISITION
An operation where a buyer becomes an owner of a good or service.

ACTIVE POPULATION
Number of persons able and wanting to work.

ADVANCED ECONOMIC INDICATOR
Index that shows variation from a recent period and usually forecasts a change in economic direction.

ASSET
A group of goods and credits that belong to an enterprise or individual.

BALANCE OF PAYMENTS
Net balance of the total economic transactions between a country and the exterior.

BANK (RESERVE) DISCOUNT RATE
The Reserve Banks' interest rate that it charges ordinary banks.

BEAR MARKET
A stock market trend of downward prices over a period.

BOND
Negotiable debt certificate issued by governments, companies, municipalities, etc. carrying a guaranty on assets of the issuer and offering interest to the buyer.

BUDGET DEFICIT
The excess of expenditures over government revenue.

BUDGET SURPLUS
Excess of government revenues over expenditures.

BUDGET
A mechanism for determining expenditures and revenues of organisations like governments, companies, etc.

BULL MARKET
A stock market trend of upward prices over a period.

BUSINESS ACQUISITION
An operation where one business buys another.

BUY OPTIONS
Right to buy during a time-period, a determined number of shares at a fixed price per option.

CAPITAL GAIN
Profit realised on the sale of a good or real estate including stocks and bonds.

CAPITAL LOSS
Loss realised on the sale of a good or stock.

CENTRAL BANK (FEDERAL RESERVE)
Government institution responsible for the issuance of money and control of credit in the country.

CLOSE
Price paid for a share on the market on the last trade of a daily session.

COMMERCIAL BALANCE

Net balance between a nation's imports and exports expressed in dollars.

COMMERCIAL DEFICIT
The excess debt between exports and imports of a country.

COMMISSION
Money paid by an investor to a broker for trading investments.

CONJECTURAL INFLATION
Inflation tied to economic cycles that provokes in the mid-term an adjustment of supply and demand.

CONSTANT DOLLARS
Measure of an economic activity expressed in money value to a reference year.

CONSUMER CREDIT CORPORATION
A business that gives short term credit.

CONSUMER PRICE INDEX
Index measuring the price trends of current goods and services essential to a family household compared to a reference year.

CREDIT
Delay in payment on a purchase or reimbursement of a debt.

CURRENT DOLLARS
Measure of an economic activity expressed in value to current year.

DEBENTURE
A type of debit issued by governments, municipal corporations, and diverse institutions and is not guaranteed by the assets of the issuer.

DEBIT
An amount of money one owes to a lending institution.

DEBT RATIO
Ratio between long-term debt of a company and its shareholders' net worth.

DEMAND DEPOSIT
A deposit that can be withdrawn without any delay or penalties.

DEMAND
Quantity of a good or service that can be bought at a fixed price.

DEVALUATION
Falling of a nation's currency compared to other nation's currencies.

DISCOUNT
Excess in the nominal value of a share to its price on the market.

DISCOUNT BROKER
A stock broker who charges less commission on market trades and offers no advice to customers.

DISCOUNT RATE
Rate where financial institutions exchange their services.

DISCOUNT TRADE
Sale or purchase of a stock inferior to its par value.

DIVIDEND
Part of a companies profit disbursed to a shareholder in money or shares.

DOW-JONES INDUSTRIAL INDEX
The New York stock exchange index representing the average prices of 30 large industrial companies.

DURABLE GOOD
A good which has a long life such as a car, appliance, furniture, etc.

EARNINGS PER SHARE
A ratio showing the net profits less privileged dividends and the total numbers of common shares.

ECONOMIC BOOM
Period of economic expansion having a very strong growth of supply and demand of goods and services.

ECONOMIC CYCLE
An economic period that consists of the phases of: expansion, overheating, recession, and recovery.

ECONOMIC DEPRESSION
Economic recession characterized by a very strong fall in the demand and supply of goods and services.

ECONOMIC EXPANSION
Phase of an economic cycle where the demand and supply of goods and services rise at a constant pace.

ECONOMIC INDICATOR
A measure of evolution of a given segment of the economy.

ECONOMIC RECOVERY (PICKUP)
Economic cycle phase during which there is a balance between supply and demand on goods and services.

EXCHANGE RATE
Comparison between the value of currencies of two countries.

EXPORTS
Sales to a foreign country of goods produced in another country.

EXTERNAL TRADE (COMMERCE)
The exchange of goods and services between a country and another (or others).

FISCAL POLICY
Practice where a government adjusts its revenue and expenditures to influence economic cycles.

FREE TRADE
Elimination or partial of trade restrictions between two countries.

FULL EMPLOYMENT
Economic situation where almost all the active, looking for work, population occupy a job.

GOOD
A material product resulting from economic activity.

GROSS DOMESTIC PRODUCT
Measure of a country's goods and services produced within the country over a given period.

IMPORTS
Purchases by a country of goods or services from others.

INFLATION
Phenomenon that inflates (increases) prices that result from an imbalance in supply and demand of goods and services in economy.

INTEREST
Cost paid by a borrower to a lender for the use of a sum of money during a given period of time.

INTERNATIONAL COMMERCE (TRADE)
The exchange of goods or services between countries.

INVESTMENT PORTFOLIO
A number of stocks, bonds, etc. held by an investor.

LIABILITY
Amount of debts and engagements owed by a business.

LIMITED PRICE ORDER
A request given to a broker to sell or buy a stock at a given price only.

LONG TERM DEBT
The part of liabilities that cannot be repaid immediately.

MACRO ECONOMICS
Study of behavior and functioning of large parts of the economy (governments, total investments, foreign trade, etc.).

MARGIN BUY
Purchase of an investment on the stock market paying a part of the cost, remainder being a credit (margin) owing to a brokerage firm.

MARGIN CALL
Obligation of an investor, on the decrease of a stock bought on margin, to reimburse his broker in part or total.

MARKET CORRECTION
A swift movement of the stock market where profits are taken by investors.

MARKET INDEX
Index representing the average prices of certain stocks.

MARKET PRICE ORDER
A request given to a broker to sell or buy a stock at the current price on the market.

MICRO ECONOMICS
Study of behavior and functioning of individual elements (families, businesses, etc.) in an economy.

MONETARY MASS
Sum of money and near liquid money circulating in an economy.

MONETARY POLICY
Practice where a government controls the money mass of a country.

MONEY MARKET
A market of cash type deposits which is traded between financial institutions.

MORTGAGE MARKET
A market where one negotiates the debts guaranteed by mortgages.

MUTUAL FUND
An institution with fixed capital that makes investments for a group of investors who have given it a sum of money.

NET PROFIT MARGIN
Ratio giving the difference between net profits and net sales.

NET PROFIT
Gain made between total expenditures and total income of an enterprise.

NOMINAL VALUE
Listed value of money in trading or loans made.

NON-DURABLE GOOD
A good which has a short life such as clothing, etc.

NYSE (NEW YORK STOCK EXCHANGE) COMPOSITE INDEX
Index representing all the stocks listed on the exchange weighted by the value of market prices.

OPEN ORDER
Request to a broker that remains valid until it is realized.

OPTIONS
Right given by a holder to sell or buy a quantity of shares at a determined price for a given period not exceeding a year.

ORDINARY GOVERNMENT BONDS
Bonds, negotiable, issued by governments with a fixed period and fixed interest rate.

PAR VALUE
Equal price of a share between its market value and face value.

PREFERENTIAL RATE
The interest rate banks give their best customers on loans.

PREMIUM TRADE
Sale or buy of a stock superior to its par value.

PREMIUM
An excess price on a share from its face value.

PRICE EARNINGS RATIO
Ratio between the price of a share and its profit.

PRICE
Market value of a good or service.

PRIVILEGED SHARE
Share offering certain rights and privileges where a dividend (non-obligatory) is fixed in advance and payable before all other dividends on common shares but does not have voting rights.

PROGRAMMED TRADING
Trades made on the stock market automatically when certain pre-established conditions react.

PUBLIC COMPANY
A company that issues shares (stocks) that trade on the stock markets.

PUBLIC DEBT
Total amount of financial obligations of a country.

REVALUATION
Increase in the value of money of a nation compared to other nation's money.

RETAIL SALES
Amount of merchandise sales made by stores of all kinds.

RETURN ON INVESTMENT RATE
Ratio between the profit and capital invested in a given time period.

RIGHTS
A consentment given to a shareholder to acquire other shares directly from a company at a price lower than the market price.

SAVINGS BOND
Bond issued by governments cashable at all times.

SELL OPTIONS
Right to sell during a time-period, a determined number of shares at a fixed price per option.

SHARE ACCOUNTING VALUE
Ratio between net worth of shareholders and number of shares in circulation.

SHARE-CUMULATIVE DIVIDEND
A privileged share having expected dividends that must be entirely disbursed prior to any dividend on common shares.

SHARE-PARTICIPATING
Privileged share giving a right to part of the net profits of a company over and above expected dividends.

SHARE-PRIVILEGED WITH VOTING RIGHTS
A preferred share having right to vote at time where a certain amount of dividends are not distributed.

SHARE-RE-PURCHASABLE
Privileged share subject to re-purchase over a period by the issuer under determined conditions.

SHARE-SUBORDINATE
A category of common share (class B) having an inferior voting right to common shares (class A).

SHARE-VARIABLE RATES
A privileged share where the dividends vary under certain determined economic conditions.

SHAREHOLDER'S NET WORTH
The difference between an asset and liability in a company per share.

SHORT TERM ASSET
Cash assets or other near liquid cash as Stocks, Bonds, etc.

SHORT TERM LIABILITIES
Debts of a short term nature that can be called immediately.

SP500 (STANDARD & POORS)
Index on the New York Exchange representing 500 listed shares: 400 industrials; 20 transports; 40 services; and 40 financial institutions.

STANDARD OF LIVING
Total goods and services that one can buy with their income.

STOCK (SECURITIES) BROKER
A member of a brokerage firm registered to trade shares on specific stock exchanges and who gives investment advice and information on various investment opportunities.

STOCK MARKET
The market where trades, buys and sells, are made in shares, bonds, etc. and is known as a Stock Exchange also.

STOCK OPTIONS
Right to sell or buy 100 shares of a company under option.

STOCK QUOTATION
Price offered or demanded by investors for a share on the market.

STOP PRICE ORDER
A request to buy or sell a stock at a certain price currently below the market price.

SUPPLY
Quantity of a good or service that can be sold on the market at a given price.

TAX SHELTER
Investment permitting an investor to obtain tax reductions.

TECHNICAL ANALYSIS
Analysis of large numbers of stock market statistical movements.

TERM (CERTIFIED) DEPOSIT
An investment in a financial institution for a fixed period of time paying higher interest than a normal savings account.

TRADE SURPLUS
Excess of a country's exports over imports.

TREASURY BONDS (BILLS)
An investment issued by the government over (3, 6, or 12 months) sold at a discount and reimbursed at face value (par).

TRUST COMPANY
An institution specializing in the administration of investments or assets for the account of others.

TSE300
Index representing 300 shares of companies of diverse economic activities on the Toronto Exchange.

UNEMPLOYMENT
The incapacity of someone desiring and able to work to find a job.

WARRANTS
A certificate issued by a company giving the right to buy shares of the company for a certain price over a fixed period.

WORKING CAPITAL
Difference between short term assets and short term liabilities.

YIELD
Revenue (profit) from a capital investment.

Statistics

Consumer Price Index Numbers (1980=100)				
Year	Canada	United States	Japan	Germany Fed. Rep.
1977	76.3	73.5	86.1	88.8
1978	83.1	79.1	89.4	91.3
1979	90.7	88.2	92.7	95.0
1980	100.0	100.0	100.0	100.0
1981	112.4	110.3	104.9	106.1
1982	124.7	117.1	107.7	111.9
1983	131.9	120.9	109.7	115.6
1984	137.6	126.1	112.1	118.4
1985	143.1	130.5	114.4	121.0
1986	148.9	133.1	115.2	120.7
Source: United Nations, Monthly Bulletin of Statistics				

Consumer Price Index Numbers (Yearly Variation in %)				
Year	Canada	United States	Japan	Germany Fed. Rep.
1978	8.9	7.6	3.8	2.7
1979	9.2	11.5	3.6	4.1
1980	10.2	13.4	7.9	5.3
1981	12.5	10.4	4.9	6.1
1982	10.9	6.1	2.7	5.4
1983	5.8	3.2	1.8	3.3
1984	4.3	4.3	2.2	2.4
1985	4.0	3.5	2.1	2.2
1986	4.1	2.0	0.7	-0.2
Source: United Nations, Monthly Bulletin of Statistics				

Unemployment Rate				
Year	Canada	United States	Japan	Germany Fed. Rep.
1977	8.1	7.0	2.0	4.6
1978	8.4	6.0	2.2	4.5
1979	7.5	5.8	2.1	4.3
1980	7.5	7.1	2.0	3.8
1981	7.5	7.6	2.2	5.5
1982	11.0	9.7	2.4	7.5
1983	11.9	9.6	2.6	9.1
1984	11.3	7.5	2.7	9.1
1985	10.5	7.2	2.6	9.3
1986	9.6	7.0	2.8	9.0
Source: United Nations, Monthly Bulletin of Statistics				

World Trade - Exports (In million US$)				
Year	Canada	United States	Japan	Germany Fed. Rep.
1977	41,876	119,005	80,493	118,070
1978	46,569	141,228	97,544	142,454
1979	56,055	178,798	103,045	171,799
1980	64,959	216,672	129,248	192,930
1981	70,018	233,739	152,016	176,043
1982	68,496	212,275	138,911	176,428
1983	73,514	200,538	146,668	169,425
1984	86,729	217,888	170,107	169,784
1985	87,479	213,146	175,683	183,406
1986	86,725	217,304	209,153	242,411
Source: United Nations, Monthly Bulletin of Statistics				

World Trade - Imports (In million US$)				
Year	Canada	United States	Japan	Germany Fed. Rep.
1977	39,808	156,758	70,797	101,430
1978	43,869	184,684	79,430	121,751
1979	53,687	220,958	110,670	159,618
1980	59,104	255,643	140,520	188,001
1981	66,303	273,352	143,288	163,934
1982	55,035	254,884	131,932	155,856
1983	61,343	269,878	126,392	152,899
1984	73,705	341,177	136,522	151,246
1985	76,413	361,626	129,480	157,645
1986	81,099	387,081	126,408	189,484
Source: United Nations, Monthly Bulletin of Statistics				

World Trade Balance (In million US$)				
Year	Canada	United States	Japan	Germany Fed. Rep.
1977	2,068	-37,753	9,696	16,640
1978	2,700	-43,456	18,114	20,703
1979	2,368	-42,160	-7,625	12,181
1980	5,855	-38,971	-11,272	4,929
1981	3,715	-39,613	8,728	12,109
1982	13,461	-42,609	6,979	20,572
1983	12,171	-69,340	20,276	16,526
1984	13,024	-123,289	33,585	18,538
1985	11,066	-148,480	46,203	25,761
1986	5,626	-169,777	82,745	52,927
Source: United Nations, Monthly Bulletin of Statistics				

Exchange Rates (National Currency per U.S. dollar)				
Year	Canada	United States	Japan	Germany Fed. Rep.
1977	1.094	1.000	240.000	2.105
1978	1.186	1.000	194.600	1.828
1979	1.168	1.000	239.700	1.731
1980	1.195	1.000	203.000	1.959
1981	1.186	1.000	219.900	2.255
1982	1.229	1.000	235.000	2.376
1983	1.244	1.000	232.200	2.724
1984	1.321	1.000	251.100	3.148
1985	1.397	1.000	200.500	2.461
1986	1.380	1.000	159.100	1.941
Source: United Nations, Monthly Bulletin of Statistics				

Market Prices of Industrial Shares (Index numbers 1980=100)				
Year	Canada	United States	Japan	Germany Fed. Rep.
1977	46.2	80.6	79.5	103.2
1978	50.6	78.9	86.9	108.2
1979	73.3	85.4	94.9	104.6
1980	100.0	100.0	100.0	100.0
1981	97.4	107.2	116.3	100.4
1982	76.8	99.3	115.8	99.0
1983	114.4	134.2	136.5	133.5
1984	110.2	134.7	172.1	150.4
1985	130.5	154.5	210.2	199.9
1986	143.9	194.9	279.2	270.4
Source: United Nations, Monthly Bulletin of Statistics				

Rates of Discount of Central Banks (End of period)				
Year	Canada	United States	Japan	Germany Fed. Rep.
1977	7.5	6.0	4.3	3.0
1978	10.8	9.5	3.5	3.0
1979	14.0	12.0	6.3	6.0
1980	17.3	13.0	7.3	7.5
1981	14.7	12.0	5.5	7.5
1982	10.3	8.5	5.5	5.0
1983	10.0	8.5	5.0	4.0
1984	10.2	8.0	5.0	4.5
1985	9.5	7.5	5.0	4.0
1986	8.5	5.5	3.0	3.5
Source: United Nations, Monthly Bulletin of Statistics				

Gross Domestic Product (Billions)				
Year	Canada	United States	Japan	Germany Fed. Rep.
	$Can	$US	Yen	D Mark
1977	217.9		184,460.0	1,200.5
1978	241.6	2,145.7	204,405.0	1,285.3
1979	276.1	2,388.4	221,546.0	1,392.3
1980	309.9	2,606.6	240,177.0	1,478.9
1981	356.0	2,934.9	257,364.0	1,540.9
1982	374.4	3,045.3	269,628.0	1,597.9
1983	405.7	3,275.7	280,256.0	1,674.8
1984	445.6	3,634.6	297,947.0	1,754.3
1985	479.4		316,114.0	1,839.9
Source: United Nations, Monthly Bulletin of Statistics				

Gross Domestic Product at Constant Prices (Billions)				
Year	Canada	United States	Japan	Germany Fed. Rep.
	1981 Can$	1975 US$	1980 Yen	1980 DM
1977	311.5	1,742.0	207,989.3	1,357.2
1978	325.8	1,784.3	204,405.0	1,285.3
1979	338.4	1,830.5	221,546.0	1,392.3
1980	343.4	1,822.5	240,177.0	1,478.9
1981	356.0	1,884.6	257,364.0	1,540.9
1982	344.5	1,828.5	269,628.0	1,597.9
1983	355.4	1,882.3	280,256.0	1,674.8
1984	377.8	2,017.1	297,947.0	1,754.3
1985	393.8		316,114.0	1,839.9
Source: United Nations, Monthly Bulletin of Statistics				

Gross Domestic Product (Rate of Growth)				
Year	Canada	United States	Japan	Germany Fed. Rep.
1978	4.6	2.4	-1.7	-5.3
1979	3.9	2.6	8.4	8.3
1980	1.5	-0.4	8.4	6.2
1981	3.7	3.4	7.2	4.2
1982	-3.2	-3.0	4.8	3.7
1983	3.2	2.9	3.9	4.8
1984	6.3	7.2	6.3	4.7
1985	4.2		6.1	4.9
Source: United Nations, Monthly Bulletin of Statistics				

Bibliography

Economics
Ninth Edition, Paul A. Samuelson, McGraw-Hill, 1973.

Microeconomics, Theory and Applications
Second Edition, Edwin Mansfield, W.W. Norton, 1975.

Towards The Next Economics and Other Essays
Peter F. Drucker
Harper & Row, 1982

Diversification Through Acquistion
Malcom S. Salter and Wolf A. Weinhold
The Fress Press, 1982.

Financial Strategy: Studies in Creation, Transfer, and Destruction of Shareholder Value
William E. Fruhan
Richard D. Irwin Press, 1979.

Guide To The Options Markets
Toronto Stock Exchange,1985.

Pocket Banker
Tim Hindle
The Economist Publications, 1987.

Money
Diane Cohen
Prentice-Hall, 1987.

Contrary Investing - Buying Low and Selling High
Richard E. Band, Penquin Books, 1986.

1987 Need Not Become 1929
Myron Magnet
Fortune, November 23, 1987.

The Day The Brokers Picked Their Own Pockets

R.L.Stern and Allan Sloan
Forbes, November 16, 1987.

Stock Market Signals To Managers
Alfred Rappaport
Harvard Business Review, Nov.-Dec. 1987.

Small Company Finance: What Books Don't Say
R.I. Levin and V.R. Travis
Harvard Business Review, Nov.-Dec. 1987.

Index

EXPRESSIONS IN ALL CAPITALS REFER TO THE DEFINITIONS'SECTION; **page numbers in boldface indicate major references into the text.**

About the Authors

About the Authors

Ruben J. Dunn is a Canadian economist. Born in 1945, he holds a Bachelor of Arts degree in Economics and a Master's degree in Economic Development Planning from the University of Montreal.

Mr. Dunn worked several years as a consultant in various fields of Economics and Finance. He is now Manager of Market planning, with Quebec-Hydro, one of the most important public utilities in North America.

John H. Morris is also a Canadian economist. He holds a Bachelor of Arts degree in Economics from the University of British Columbia and a Master of Business Administration from the same university.

Mr. Morris, who is 44 years old, has been employed with several federal Canadian Government departments as a Financial Analyst and as a Senior Economist in Ottawa, Ontario. Since 1980 he has acted as Economist and Financial Advisor for Quebec-Hydro in Montreal.